THE HARD FACTS ABOUT SOFT SKILLS

BY: RICHARD A. CELESTIN, ESQ.

To Mom and Dad for always believing in me.
To Steve for being a dynamic and inspiring big brother
and role model.
To Elizabeth, Jaden, and Justin for being my foundation
and dealing with my madness.
To Alexis for being there for me no matter what.
To Nikka for being my spiritual guide and supporting
friend.
To Ify, Tanya, and Charles for pushing me to achieve
new levels of success.
To Tariq for being a mentor, advisor and birthday
brother.
To every professional who helped me grow, mature, and
discover my potential.
To every person who doubted me, hated on me, and
wished me failure.

To every young person with whom I have ever had the
pleasure of working with, educating, learning from,
inspiring, being inspired by, uplifting, and empowering.

Thank you.

TABLE OF CONTENTS

PREFACE

"Successful and unsuccessful people do not vary greatly
in their abilities. They vary in their desires
to reach their potential."
– John Maxwell

Professionalism is a fluid concept. We often
think of professionalism and automatically think of
clothing. We can envision a guy dressed sharply in a
suit, tie and dress shoes. But professionalism is way
more than the clothes you wear. Webster's Dictionary
defines professionalism as the competence or skill
expected of a professional. It also includes the mentality,
the confidence, and the presentation of a person. We
must all take a step back from our assumptions and look
at professionalism as a lifestyle- one necessary to
achieve success.

As you navigate life and the professional world it
is easy to see that in order to be successful one must
possess a strong mental component as well as a physical
one. Success is a package deal- the combination of the
strategic and methodical planning and focus combined
with the physical presence and presentation. Each aspect
requires understanding, attention, respect and practice in
order to truly get a sense of how to utilize these skills to
your potential and to your advantage. While one may
never be able to truly master the essence of
professionalism, as you move closer to knowing and
understanding the mental and physical components of it,
the more you move closer to achieving greatness.

Occasionally I hear some complaints when discussing a transition into the professional world and what is needed to succeed in it. Why do I need to change who I am to get ahead? Am I selling out? The truth is no one is asking you to change who you are as a person. The person you are just adds some originality and spice to the professional you will become. In order to be successful at whatever you do you have to know the game, understand the rules for that game, and play it better than anyone and everyone else.

You can't play basketball following the rules of football. You can't expect to do well in science class if you are following along in your history textbook. The professional world is no different. It operates under a different set of rules and expectations than the outside world. If you do not know the rules and play the game, your chances of being successful become much harder. To be in the game, you have to know the game and the rules. To win the game, you have to play it and play it very well. This doesn't mean you need to become a robot. You bring who you are as a person everywhere you go. We will explore the different ways you can add your own touch to make yourself unique while also working on mastering the game and embodying professionalism.

As a consumer, when presented with a book or workshop or seminar, I find myself asking the same questions- what makes you qualified to do this, why are you doing this, and what is your endgame or ultimate goal in doing this. Assuming you, as the consumer, have the same questions, I will make it a point to answer them.

In the various roles I have played as a professional in the past 12 years, whether it is in the capacity of a lawyer, a professor, a consultant in an educational setting, or as an entrepreneur, I have encountered so many people ranging in age, experiences, dreams, goals and plans. In some instances, I have taken on the role of educator and in others I find myself in a position of student, even from the very young population I work with. I have noted the things that make people strong and focused as well as areas that are needed for improvement and strengthening. I have done countless workshops focused on these topics and decided that while I can only do so much with the time I have, a book can reach greater audiences.

The goal of this book is to educate and empower young and pre-professionals as they begin to embark on the journey of professional growth. I also recognize that this book can be powerful for experienced professionals who want to learn how to advance in their career. I want readers of this book to gain insight into some of the skills that are rarely spoken about but expected in a professional setting. Knowledge is power and I am hoping this book is a source of power for anyone who picks it up.

On a much more personal level, and for the purposes of full transparency and honesty, I never liked school and rarely did well in school. I knew that if I placed all of my future goals and aspirations on my ability to focus and do well in school that I would be setting myself up for failure. I needed to discover and develop an aspect of my persona and my brand that would allow me to navigate through life knowing that I may not be the smartest person in the room but I would always find a way to get the job done well and in a respected fashion. I became a student of life at a young age, learning from anyone who I interacted with or had an opportunity to observe. I began to notice some of the unique aspects of people's approach to human interactions that gave them advantages and set them apart from the pack. I had no clue at the time that I was actually learning about soft skills and their incredible value. I would be doing a great disservice if I did not share all that I have learned, the skills I learned through trial and error and failure, and the path that I navigated to reach the level of success that I have earned to date.

Despite being a professional and an entrepreneur, I recognize that I am not an expert on all things professionalism related. In recognizing my shortcomings, I knew I could not truly write this book and present multiple approaches and opinions on the matter alone. As a result, I enlisted the support of some of the most professional, hard-working, successful people in my circle. Some I observed, noting their calculated movement, others I gained insight from the information they would share, and others I asked to provide me with their insight and experiences so I can share it with you. Imagine the amazing minds of almost two dozen professionals in various areas of work providing insight and advice to support your professional journey?

This book is not meant to be an end-all, be-all book on all things soft skills related. My goal is to lay a foundation, and to spark interest in, the skills necessary to achieve success as YOU define it. A true seeker of success will continue the research and the journey of self-development and exploration and discover their strengths, the skills needed, and what is necessary to grow as a person.

CHAPTER 1

WHY SOFT SKILLS MATTER

"The mark of higher education isn't the knowledge you
accumulate in your head.
It's the skills you gain about how to learn."
- Adam Grant

As a professional, educator and employer, I have
seen just about everything. I have interacted with
professionals who were incapable of communicating
thoughts and ideas effectively. I have taught college
students who did not have a resume developed. I have
shaken the hands of individuals in a professional setting
and was left wondering if that was a handshake or a
lifeless limb. I have interviewed potential candidates for
a position who openly expressed that their biggest
weakness was their ability to arrive to work on time. I
have shared business cards with people I have met at
events only to receive an e-mail, sometimes the same
day, requesting a job or some other type of favor. I have
supervised interns who had to be told every other minute
what to do otherwise they would get lost on social
media.

After each and every of these situations, as well
as the numerous more that I cannot even begin to
explain, I am left wondering one simple question- how?
How is it that there are so many individuals who lack
some of these essential core skills? How is one able to
progress in a professional setting without mastering, or
at least understanding, some of these skills? It is in this
train of thought that I have come to realize that soft

1

skills are both under-respected and under-appreciated by too many. I feel this is true on a greater scale with the youth today, as technology advances do not require a focus on these skills and schools are too overwhelmed with meeting standards to properly educate students on these matters. While I feel an attempt should be made to address the important nature of soft skills in adults who may lack them, I choose to focus on young people, this world's future professionals, to shed some light and impart some insight and advice.

So, what exactly are soft skills? Soft skills are those unique talents and abilities that make up some of the most important and required qualities that a future professional can have. Unlike hard skills, which are technical and tangible skills learned through education and experience and can be defined and measured, soft skills are intangible attributes of a person, often related to their behavior and disposition. This can include punctuality, ability to multi-task, creative thinking and communication skills. This goes far deeper than just simply focusing on the technical skills of a person but investigating a person's personality and mindfulness. There is no way to quantify how much or many soft skills a person possesses. This is often determined by numerous approaches, actions, and reactions that a person demonstrates under certain circumstances.

Examples of HARD SKILLS	Examples of SOFT SKILLS
-Degree or certificate	-Communication
-Dual Language Fluency	-Flexibility
-Typing speed	-Leadership
-Computer programming	-Teamwork
-Machine operation	-Problem Solving Abilities

To get a greater sense of how critical soft skills are, take a look at a posting for employment and focus on the qualifications required for the position. After laying out the educational and technical experience needed (hard skills), most employers seek a candidate that has "excellent communication skills", is a "team player", can "work both independently as well as in a group setting", and has "strong organizational skills", to name a few. Interestingly enough, some would say these are the essential skills of a leader. For someone not seeking employment but rather a student in a school, these characteristics, if laid out in a letter of recommendation, could be the difference maker in whether you are considered by a school for enrollment.

A person's qualifications, education or technical skills are not to be dismissed at all. The point is that of equal importance, and arguable more importance, and often overlooked, are soft skills. In order to achieve any level of success, it is important to develop all aspects of your brand. With each tool understood and mastered, you enter new phases of your life equipped with a wide array of skills that can adapt to almost any set of circumstances. As schools and employment become more competitive to enter, it will be these intangible skills that will serve as the difference in potential candidates. If all of this is in fact accurate, it leaves one wondering why there is not a greater emphasis on teaching soft skills, particularly to younger generations? The problem, in my opinion and from a very simplistic view, lies in the current school model as well as the advancements in technology.

Prior to becoming a vendor with the Department of Education over eight years ago, I had no real insight into how schools operated and the demands placed on administrators. Through my work I have discovered how overwhelming a burden Principals, Assistant Principals and teachers have in meeting increasing demands while receiving less resources. The need to produce above-standard results on evaluations and student performances on standardized exams have teachers constantly teaching towards a test, leading to a tremendous emphasis on exam scores. This leaves little room to educate young students on the importance of soft skills.

All too often I have encountered students who are excelling in terms of academics but lack social skills and assertiveness. I have encountered students who struggle academically but possess all the charm, personality and presence you would want in an employee, an employer, or a leader. Schools are the perfect arena to introduce and address the need for soft skills. Students must understand that having the highest grades may get you into that college or land you the job you want, but it will take those soft skills to maintain that position and continue to grow professionally.

One of the greatest strengths of this younger generation also happens to be partly to blame for creating one of the greatest weaknesses as well-technology. While there is a great proficiency for understanding, managing and developing technology, it has also created a disconnect in learning how to develop personal and social connections. Young people laugh when I tell them that as a teenager texting and e-mailing were not options. We had to (brace yourself) actually talk to people, whether in person or (brace yourself again) over the phone. Developing communication skills

4

was not optional. Today, young people spend more and more time behind a screen and less and less time identifying and developing the essential soft skills related to becoming successful professionals. One can argue that each generation has faced its obstacles in developing soft skills. However, with the insane popularity of smart phones, social media and gaming platforms, the hurdles are greater today than ever before.

Rather than approach a discussion about soft skills from a "list and explain" viewpoint, I instead want to discuss soft skills and how they tie into a path of success. This transitions the conversation from identifying a group of skills to how to develop and use these skills in order to be successful in your personal and professional goals. Soft skills should not be viewed as independent and unconnected attributes but instead characteristics and qualities essential to navigate through life's challenges and obstacles while growing and becoming a stronger and better you. Each soft skill overlaps with another and together represent the key ingredients to achieving success.

CHAPTER 2

PROFESSIONALISM

"Professionalism: It's NOT the job you DO,
It's HOW you DO the job."
- Anonymous

The concept of professionalism has long been the standard for the actions, qualities and characteristics of professionals. It is less about the type of profession you are in, the type of workplace you are part of, and the title you hold than it is about how you conduct yourself under your circumstances. I have long thought that the concept of professionalism should apply to students, even though they do not have a specific profession. Or do they?

For any pre-professionals reading this and wondering, let me be clear: being a student is a profession. As a student, you are tasked with expectations and responsibilities that ultimately (and hopefully) lead to your success and promotion to the next level of academia, or to the actual professional world. Students spend five days a week, 25+ hours generally, towards mastering a single craft- how to be a good student. I can still hear my father's voice in my head when I came home with a failing grade or some other type of negative note- "I work 2-3 jobs so that you can have what you need in order to focus on the only thing that should matter to you right now- being a good student".

So, if students are in fact members of a profession, then the standards and expectations of professionalism should apply, right? The truth is that when you look at what encompasses professionalism, such standards should be expected of students on a daily basis in order to prepare them for the world that awaits them. By not doing so, we are doing a tremendous disservice to these future professionals.

Professionalism is all about presentation. It is about how you conduct yourself during important matters. While there are several important qualities that exemplify professionalism, I want to focus on four that are particularly relevant and critical for professionals to understand and master - demeanor, accountability, work ethic and honesty.

DEMEANOR

Your demeanor includes both your behavior towards others as well as the manner in which you carry that out. It is essentially how you approach different situations. Are you the type to be calm when the pressure is on or do you freak out? Are you able to maintain your composure when someone questions or challenges you or do you lose it? As a solid professional, and someone who can be characterized as a leader, it is essential to maintain a confident, cool-headed, and positive demeanor. You must be consistent in your attitude and your approach to problems while also finding a way to keep your emotions in check.

Your demeanor will constantly be tested based on the circumstances that you are placed in as well as the people that you are interacting with. Knowing and understanding this means you cannot be surprised when an unforeseen challenge happens. Instead, you have to work to be prepared for it. You cannot choose who your classmates will be, nor your co-workers, nor the people you will interact with on a daily basis. You are not going to like everybody and, honestly, not everybody is going to like you. Not knowing what you will encounter when you meet people under different circumstances is exactly why maintaining a steady demeanor and approach using a systematic formula is critical.

Due to the various areas that I find myself working in, whether it be in a courtroom or in a classroom, I have encountered all types of people with all types of demeanors, attitudes, and behaviors. I could not effectively do my job, nor maintain my sanity, if my demeanor constantly was swayed easily with each encounter. Instead, I have developed a mantra which generally consists of three things to remind myself so I stick to my demeanor and get the job done.

1. **Don't take it personal**. Often times people are not happy or have a negative demeanor due to circumstances that have nothing to do with me. Yet I am the one who feels the brunt of that negative force. I have to remind myself that it is not my fault and that my objective is to help and to learn.

2. **Keep calm – I'm a Professional**. By keeping calm, I put my emotions under control which allows me to maintain my positive and controlled demeanor. Whether it is through deep breaths or taking a step back to process, the goal is to remain calm despite the circumstances. Even in times where I am super nervous or anxious, I remember that those are internal

feelings that should be kept internal and I have to exude a calm demeanor.

3. **Find the positive in all things**. Even in the toughest situation, there is a way to find some type of positive to focus on. It is important to find that positive source and use it as a strength as well as an anchor to keep you centered. By floating into the realm of negativity it will affect your attitude, your emotions as well as your thought process- none of which will lead to anything positive.

Confidence is also a huge aspect of your demeanor. When you exude confidence, it draws people to you and commands their attention and respect. The more a person looks like they believe in themselves the more you will be open to believing in them. Sometimes a confident demeanor is a front to hide nerves or anxiousness which is completely fine. If you think and act confidently, despite having doubts initially, you will fall in line with that mentality and everything will align itself. Some people may dislike you for exuding confidence which is often a personal issue for them and should not affect your confidence in yourself. Keep in mind, as it is notoriously known, that there is a fine line between confidence and conceit.

ACCOUNTABILITY

When I am asked what it takes to become a lawyer, I recount the exhausting process of classes, exams, applications, sacrifices and years of school that stand in the way of a Juris Doctorate. However, I always mention afterwards that as difficult as it was to obtain such a prestigious degree, losing it, and the privileges that come with it, is substantially easier. This is the case because lawyers, as with all professionals, are held accountable for their actions and are thus obligated to take responsibility for their actions, particularly when they are negative or harmful. Accountability is key to professionalism.

One of the more challenging aspects of establishing accountability is the ease with which people are able to blame others. If you talk to the right person nothing is their fault and everything is the fault of someone or anyone else. The truth is accountability starts with you. You must take responsibility for your actions and decisions. You are placed in the driver's seat of your life and are tasked with making the decisions that will affect what direction you go in.

If you choose not to study and fail an exam you can certainly blame the teacher, the exam, the textbook, the lunar cycle, the breakfast you had that morning, etc. If you procrastinate on completing a project due to procrastination you can blame anyone and anything that comes to mind as well. At the end of the day the fault lies squarely on you. Take ownership of your work and understand that you are accountable first and foremost for your failures as well as your successes.

One of the greatest pitfalls of failing to be accountable is entering into a spectator approach to life. As a spectator, much like at sporting events, you sit and watch. You can root and cheer and sigh but you ultimately just watch. You may watch opportunities pass you by or watch failures come one after the other. The risk at that point is to enter into a mentality where you just accept failure and believe that maybe you are cursed or jinxed. However, someone who takes ownership of the situation transitions from a spectator to an active player. The mindset shifts from someone watching things go wrong to someone figuring out why things are going wrong and trying to fix them.

Only after you have understood the importance of holding yourself accountable, and putting it into practice, are you then tasked with the next difficult step- holding other people accountable. This ties more into when you are placed in a leadership role. It is critical to remember, however, that you cannot hold anyone else to a standard that you do not hold yourself to. By demonstrating a sense of responsibility for your own actions, you will be better placed in a position to lead others and have a dialogue about holding others responsible. Any good professional is always observing and learning; raise people's expectations of you and themselves by establishing and demonstrating the standard and not just talking about it.

To be honest, it is incredibly difficult to consistently hold ourselves accountable because we are only human and we make mistakes. This is why I always recommend to people that they find an accountability coach. An accountability coach will hold you accountable when you fail to do so. If you set a deadline and give yourself a break, a coach will reinforce the importance of the deadline. However, you must be careful in selecting the right coach, as they must first value and understand the importance of accountability to ensure their advice is followed by anyone else.

WORK ETHIC

"Work ethic" seems to be a popular buzz phrase when it comes to most professional and educational settings. We are often asked to, or expected to, demonstrate a strong work ethic. I have heard people define work ethic as simply working hard. It is more complex than that. It involves the principles and morals you use when completing a task or approaching your job. It is how you define your attitude and behavior when it comes to carrying out your work-related responsibilities. Simply saying you are a hard working does not demonstrate or define your work ethic. Being able to demonstrate your morals and principles when it comes to how you approach and value your work lays the proper foundation.

What exactly encompasses a strong work ethic? There are several aspects of a strong work ethic that are considered valuable in a professional and educational setting. In my opinion, the key elements about which I will go into further detail on are integrity, quality of work, discipline and teamwork.

1. **Integrity**. Every aspect of who you are and how you approach your work should be encompassed with integrity. It is a major component of your character and how you define yourself as a trustworthy and reliable person. This means doing the right thing, no matter what, at all times, even when no one is watching. It is also a critical ingredient in developing and earning the trust and faith of your co-workers by living your values and principles in the relationships you have.

2. **Quality of Work**. Simply completing a project or a task should not be the ultimate goal. It should be completing a project or task to the best of your ability and taking great pride in the quality of your work. How you complete a task, as well as the finished product, define your work ethic. If you view your work as a representation of who you are, then this should raise your level of expectation for your work.

3. **Discipline**. Starting and ending a task, despite temptations, distractions, and frustrating interruptions, requires discipline. It is essentially a set of internal rules that you must establish and hold true to in order to stay focused on a given task. If you have a task or a goal then you must do what is needed to see it through. Lack of discipline is often the underlying reasons why so many people fail to achieve goals and aspirations.

4. **Teamwork**. Working in a team is often a big fear that many people share. The need to share responsibility, deal with complex personalities, or find a way to come to a consensus on what needs to be done can be very challenging. While it is certainly a challenge, it is also a great opportunity to grow as a person and develop and strengthen new skills. Considering that most professional and educational settings will involve working with multiple people, the ability to work within a group setting (whether as a leader or a supporter) is an essential skill and one

that is highly sought after in the professional world.

A strong work ethic is invaluable, not only in your present position but in your future goals as well. In the professional world, your work ethic becomes part of your reputation and ultimately how people know and define you. A strong work ethic will open doors for you, with plenty of people ready to support your journey to greater achievements. A poor work ethic, however, can cost you opportunities and will linger like a stigma or stain.

HONESTY

Although self-explanatory, and hopefully automatic, it is important to stress the importance of honesty when discussing professionalism. Honesty truly is the best policy. By demonstrating that you are an honest person, you instill trust and faith in others. No one wants to work with someone that is dishonest and untrustworthy.

In addition to being honest in your actions, it is equally as important to be honest with your co-workers and, depending on your role or position, your staff. Honestly does not have to be mean and brutal but can be, and should be, constructive. The goal of honesty is to strengthen and uplift as opposed to break down.

Professionalism is a fluid concept and encompasses so many attributes and character traits that are all connected and related in some way or another. The foundation of it all is to approach your work with greater care and respect than simply aiming to just complete a task to get it over with and done. It is also important to remember that your level of professionalism remains with you as you navigate the professional world.

CHAPTER 3

MENTALITY OF SUCCESS

"Your attitude, not your aptitude,
will determine your altitude."
- Zig Ziglar

Despite how you define success, most would agree that the idea of being successful involves some type of tangibility to it. It may be the big house and fancy cars, or the vast amount of wealth, or the movies and/or books that feature that person. However, what is impossible to see but remains one of the most critical and challenging aspects of success is the mental aspect. It is easy to see what success looks like but it is difficult to imagine the level of mental strength and focus that is required to reach that level of success. The truth is that no matter how hard you work the true key to success is having the mentality of success.

To be honest, this aspect of success was by far the most challenging for me to understand, appreciate and apply. It is also one that I am constantly aware of and invest time and energy to continue developing. As a result of suffering intense bullying in school as a child, along with being overweight, my self-esteem was always in the gutter. I rarely felt worthy of attention or acclaim. This feeling extended into my adulthood where I would not know how to accept compliments or felt that I was deserving of praise. The turning point for me, however, was when I developed a mentality of success. Specifically, I developed a better understanding of my purpose and my value which resulted in a boost in my self-esteem. While the journey was very difficult and exhausting, I can share the four areas that truly made the greatest impact on my mental growth.

WHAT, WHY AND HOW

The concept of success is one in which I believe most people want to achieve. Whether it is within a profession or overall as a professional, success is often the bar which we set for ourselves to know that we have accomplished something great. However, success is not defined uniformly. We are each responsible for defining what success looks like to us. In order to develop our own definition of success, as well as develop and understand what is required to reach that success, we must ask ourselves three questions- what, why and how?

WHAT are your goals? In order to define success, you need to know what you are working towards so you have something to measure success by. Not having a clear-cut definition or success, or what our goals are, can leave us working frantically with no direction and no focus. You must explore how you define success and what that will look like to you. Defining success must be a journey of self-exploration. You should not take on other people's definition of success and adapt it as your own. Once you have this definition, as well as the goals you seek to achieve success, it is important to write them down and keep them visible. You want to constantly remind yourself of what you are working towards. You can obviously update and make changes to them but you must remember that every day is an opportunity to move one step closer to your definition of success.

WHY are you aiming for those goals and that definition of success? We live in a time that I like to call the "cut and paste" era. People's opinions, goals, and morals are cut and paste from other people's opinions, goals, and morals and adapted and shared as their own. The quickest way to start a debate is to ask someone why they have taken that position because the answer is very difficult to accept. You must develop your own "why" when it comes to guiding you through the journey of success. Your "why" should not be based on anyone else. You have to have your own internal motivation to keep you focused and determined when things get incredibly difficult and the idea of quitting seems so appealing. The answer to the question "why" is what will get you up in the morning, get you through the day, keep you on track when distractions arise, and keep that fire inside you burning as you work towards your goals.

HOW are you going to achieve those goals? At this point you should have a destination set and your reason(s) why you want to get to that destination. The question that remains is how are you going to get there? This is where developing a solid plan of action comes into play. Imagine setting a goal of starting a new business, writing a book or obtaining a scholarship. That is excellent. Now what are you going to do to achieve that goal? What actions are required? What sacrifices are needed? What will be your daily, weekly and monthly objectives? How will you measure success? If you are not meeting your benchmarks, how will you adjust to get on the right track? Formulating this plan will guide you through the process of achieving your goals and achieving success.

Do not oversimplify these three questions or the responses to them. If you want to achieve success that badly, and want to reach your goals that desperately, then the answers to these questions will require the time, energy and care that they deserve.

CHECKERS vs. CHESS

Growing up, I dominated in checkers. Between my brother and my sister, I was able to win a majority of games. One board game I avoided regularly was chess. My reasoning was usually that it was too difficult and complex or required me to think too much. It was not until I reach young adulthood that I started to truly learn how to play the game, understand the techniques involved, and respect the complexity that underlined every single move. I then realized that chess was so much more than a board game but it was a recipe for success in life. I have since modeled my life after the game of chess.

Checkers, while being an entertaining game, is a very basic one as well. Depending on which rules you play by (which can often lead to some heated arguments), you essentially have to jump your opponent's pieces while moving in only one direction and remove them from the board. Of course, reaching the opposite side of the board and getting "kinged" is always a plus. The ultimate goal is to remove all of your opponent's pieces from the board. It's pretty straight forward, without too much planning or strategy involved. Chess, however, is a whole other animal. There are six different types of pieces, each with their own movement options including forward and back movements, with the goal of trapping the opponent's king and declaring checkmate. The strategy, planning, and care that goes into each move, as well as each sacrifice to get ahead, are things of beauty. So how do you translate a board game into life?

Similar to chess, each move you make in life has to be calculated and with purpose. There should be no wasted movements- each move should serve a greater purpose and gets you one step closer to winning the game. To be successful at chess, you cannot just simply focus on your move at that time but must also consider several moves in advance as well as the anticipated moves of your opponent. Sometimes in order to advance or achieve a goal you have to take a step back, sacrifice your position, and re-think before moving forward. Every movement on the board has one of two goals- to chase down your objective and to protect what matters to you most in order to achieve success. And you thought this was just a board game? It is so much more than that if you look a little closer.

I apply a chess mentality in every aspect of my professional career. I make movements that I know are going to lead to results and get me one step closer to achieving a goal and reaching success. I am meticulous about planning and anticipating the "what if's" in a scenario. Sometimes I will do a program at no cost or a workshop with no fee knowing that it will ultimately lead to greater opportunities. The funny thing is I can now easily recognize those people with a checkers mentality and those with a chess mentality. I can differentiate between liner thinkers and those who are ready for whatever comes their way. Developing a chess mentality gives you an amazing foundation to build success upon.

READY, WILLING AND CONFIDENT

Self-confidence is a game changer. It is an incredibly powerful tool to have in your arsenal that will do amazing things in your journey to success. Being confident in who you are as a person and what you are capable of achieving attracts people and opportunities that will strengthen who you are and take you to higher levels you need to become successful. A confident person inspires confidence in others. However, a lack of self-confidence can feel overwhelming. As strong as confidence can be in a person, it is also very fragile and must be protected and strengthened constantly.

Your level of self-confidence can show in many ways. It can be seen in your behavior, your body language, how you speak, what you have to say, and many other factors that we may not even be aware of. A person who demonstrates strong self-confidence is more likely to receive the faith and trust of their audience than someone who lacks self-confidence and seems unsure of themselves. I have seen this countless times when it comes to presentations or workshops. Presenters who lack confidence are ignored or dismissed while confident speakers command the attention of everyone in the room. The more you appear to believe in yourself, particularly in the way you carry and present yourself, the more others will believe in you too.

Developing your self-confidence is easier said than done but certainly not impossible. You must do a lot of self-reflection and analysis to build your confidence. While there are many approaches and insights as to how to develop self-confidence, I think one of the most valuable pieces of advice I have ever gotten (while work on my own self-confidence issues) was to understand, appreciate, and hold others accountable to your own value. If you know, understand, and appreciate how valuable you are and what you bring to the table you not only boost your self-esteem but also create a standard which you must hold others to when they interact or do business with you. This has not only been the key to developing my self-confidence but has also been a driving force behind my own success.

One thing that people often neglect to do is to take a moment and celebrate their own accomplishments and successes. We often find ourselves moving forward and only seeking the next goal or accomplishment. It is important to stop every once in a while and look at where you are and pat yourself on the back. Take time to celebrate what you have accomplished and the obstacles you had to overcome to reach that point. The goal of this is to understand that you are valuable and have every reason in the world to have a high confidence level.

EMBRACE FAILURE

It is interesting to hear when people say that they do everything they possibly can to avoid failure. While I agree that the approach makes logical sense, it is also in conflict with the premise that failure is the catalyst to success. Some of the greatest lessons that we can ever learn will come from failure as opposed to success. And to be honest, we all experience failure at least one point in time in our lives. The question is what do you do when you fail? It is not the time to hide in a corner or to throw in the towel and quit. It is a time to embrace failure- understand why it happened, understand what changes need to be made, and develop a new plan of action to ensure success.

Walt Disney was fired from the Kansas City Star because his editor felt he lacked imagination. Oprah Winfrey was fired from her first television job and told that being on television was not the thing for her. Thomas Edison was told by his teachers that he was too stupid to learn anything. J.K. Rowling was a single mom on welfare and almost homeless when she began writing the Harry Potter series. Jay Z could not get any record label to sign him and ultimately sold his CD's out of the trunk of his car. Michael Jordan was cut by his high school basketball team.

Needless to say, the individuals mentioned above only represent a small number of people who, despite the failures and obstacles they endured in their lives, succeeded anyway. You must develop resilience in the face of failure. You have to bounce back when you get knocked down and fight ten times harder when you get back up. Failure is a part of life and it will happen over and over again. Understanding that failure is part of life, and also understanding that there should not be a single thing that can or should stop you from achieving your dreams, you will become mentally stronger and ready to handle life's challenges.

A mentality of success is the fuel that drives the vehicle. It is an essential component to achieving your goals and reaching the level of success you define for yourself. When you are mentally strong and focused, there is little in this world that can stop you.

CHAPTER 4

CIRCLE OF SUCCESS

"Your friends should motivate and inspire you. Your
circle should be well-rounded and supportive. Keep it
tight. Quality over quantity, always!"
- Anonymous

The saying goes that you can tell a lot about a
person by looking at his or her friends and who they
choose to associate with. Like-minded individuals,
whether seeking success or an excuse to be
unproductive, always seem to find each other and stick
together. In the age of social media, where it is easy to
be misguided about who our true friends are, the
definition of a friend has been confused. The people we
seek to associate ourselves with often appease a need for
fitting in or being cool more than the greater sense of
having a support group or accountability coaches.

The bottom line is clear- in order to achieve the
level of success that you want, expect, and demand of
yourself, you must look at your circle as part of that
process.

Many would argue that how smart you are, how
talented you are, where you were born, and/or your
family environment may all play some role in how
successful you will ultimately become. I argue that the
people you surround yourself with, and your circle of
success, play a much greater role. The company you
keep can affect your way of thinking and ultimately help
or hinder your ability to create a mindset for success.
Ultimately, we become more like the people that we

hang out with. We may not realize it initially, it may not be done consciously, but the role that our circle plays on us is greater than we know or may want to acknowledge.

How often do you do an accounting of the people in your circle? We sometimes spend countless hours surrounded by the same company and never really take time to analyze who they are and the roles they play. Do they elevate you or bring you down? Do they motivate and inspire you or do they discourage you and doubt you? Are they proactive people that make things happen or do they sit back, let life happen, and criticize everything when things don't go their way? By answering these questions, we can get a better sense of our circle.

When discussing this topic with people I conduct an exercise. I have them imagine their circle- whether it be friends, family, or significant others. Once this image is clear, I ask a simple question- who is the smartest, hardest working, most determined and focused person in your circle? If the answer is you, then it is time to re-evaluate your circle. I am all about serving and leading but if there is no one for you to learn from and strive to follow then you are giving and not receiving from that set of relationships.

There should always be someone in your circle who you can look to for guidance, support and possible mentorship. There should always be someone who will motivate you when you lack the will or desire to be productive. There should always be someone who believes in you and your abilities when you feel weak and decide to question them. A circle of friends that distract you, discourage you, or drains you is no circle of "friends" you want to be a part of.

What happens when a person in our circle is poisonous or draining? Ultimately, we control the influence a person plays in our lives. We can control the volume and we can control what channel we want to focus on. You cannot be afraid to cut a person from your life, or at least place them at arms-length, when you identify them as someone who is not contributing positively to your life. This is not easy because we often worry about the other person's feelings, sometimes before protecting our own feelings. However, if you truly want to achieve success you must understand that you cannot allow anyone to get in the way of your plan and your desire. Manage the volume and control the distance at all times.

FOUR TYPES OF FRIENDS YOU DON'T WANT IN YOUR CIRCLE

It is difficult to attempt to categorize all people you could potentially meet in your life into neat and clear categories. With so many different possible characteristics, traits and backgrounds it is almost impossible. However, based on what I have heard from others, as well as my own struggles in constantly working on and improving my circle, I have identified what I believe to be the 4 most notorious types of "friends" that you do not want in your circle. They are as follows:

The Battery Drainer Friend – If you imagine your body, mind and energy as functioning off a battery, you can imagine how important it is for your battery to be fully charged, or at least have enough juice to handle the daily battles we plan for and those we don't expect. The person in your circle who constantly drains your battery is someone who is dangerous. This is the type of person who likes to take but not give. This person is constantly seeking advice but never willing to give any. This person expects you to listen to any and all issues that may arise in their life but will not take the time to be a listener to your issues. This person can end up draining your battery regularly, leaving you running on fumes when it is time to focus on you and what needs to get done. You must always remember to protect your battery and your energy.

The World is Miserable Friend – This is the type of friend that will find any reason to complain about something. This person constantly seems to be surrounded by anger and frustration. And as the saying goes, misery loves company. Because they cannot seem to resolve their own issues they tend to lash out at the people closest to them, regardless of who/what the source of the problem is. This type of person is surrounded by negativity and tries to spread their negativity to anyone around them. Your frame of mind is something that must always be positive. You must always be forward thinking and envision productive and positive results in your actions and investments. There is no room for negativity or doubt. You must deflect the negativity energy, as well as the source, to avoid it influencing your focus.

The Jealous Friend – A jealous friend is very difficult to identify as they look and sound like any other friend for the most part. In reality, this is the type of friend who wishes they could be you. This person secretly admires your life and does not know how to applaud your accomplishments or cheer for your success because they envy you. This type of friend is also affectionately known as a "hater". As this type of friend is difficult to identify, the best practice is to generally be protective of your plan for success. My mother always used to tell me not to let other people know about my plans because I never knew who would be wishing failure on me. As a result, I only share my goals with people I know I can truly trust to protect my interests and support me unconditionally. Jealous friends will always be a part of your life. The better you do in life, the more jealous friends you will have. Just be mindful and protect your dreams.

The Yes Person – A "yes" person is someone who agrees with you all the time. Any ideas, any plans, any course of action is supported by this person. This may sound like the characteristics of a perfect friend but it is actually not. You do not want someone who's going to blindly approve of all of your decisions and actions. Any good friend will be open and honest with you, while also being respectful and constructive about what you are doing wrong. We naturally seek approval for our decisions so I can understand the appeal of a friend like this. However, what is most needed is someone who can help us analyze our thought processes or call us out when we need it the most.

As I have grown professionally, I have taken a harder and more critical view of the people around me. I have found myself distancing myself from unproductive, unfocused people and gravitating towards determined, motivated, and ambitious people. At times I feel guilty for taking this stance but I try to remember that it is not being done for personal reasons. The growing pains associated with personal and professional transitions are not always fun but they can be incredibly rewarding to those that understand and appreciate the big picture.

CHAPTER 5

CRITICAL THINKING AND PROBLEM SOLVING

"We are approaching a new age of synthesis.
Knowledge cannot be merely a degree or a skill... it
demands a broader vision, capabilities in critical
thinking and logical deduction without which we cannot
have constructive progress."
- Li Ka-shing

Times have changed significantly from when I
was a child. Although it may not seem like it was that
long ago, the changes and advances in education and
technology in particular have changed the scope of how
young people should learn and what they should focus
on in order to be successful. We have evolved from not
having cell phones to relying on smart phones that have
access to a massive amount of information. The job
market is transitioning from manufacturing-based to a
heavy service-orientated industry. Education has
transitioned into focusing on heavy test-prep and
standardized exams, which many argue are killing
students' ability to be creative. Whether we like or
disagree with these changes they are here and will
continue to happen. The question at hand is what can
and should be done by future professionals to prepare
for these changes and the ones to come.

Without a doubt there is a growing demand and
expectation for students and young professionals to
possess arguably two of the most important and needed
skills- critical thinking and problem solving. It is crucial
to develop and effectively apply critical thinking skills
on various levels- from personal decisions and academic

studies, to problem solving on both a personal and professional level.

As a lawyer and entrepreneur, I can honestly say that critical thinking is my most valued skill and one that is used in just about every aspect of my life. We are all inundated with information, whether as students, as users of the internet, or as new entrants into the professional world. To be successful, it is important to think critically about all of the information presented as well as to identify, evaluate, and solve complex problems and make complex decisions on a daily basis.

What exactly is critical thinking? As this is a complex concept there are various definitions that are all built on a similar premise; it is an objective, or unbiased, analysis of facts and circumstances to form a judgment or make a decision. It is taking an honest and often difficult view of issues and problems from all angles before planning a course of action. This skill is so important because it goes well beyond the ability to know or retain information but delves into how to process, analyze, and understand that information. Key tasks of a critical thinker include:

- Focusing on the most relevant information in that particular circumstance
- Understanding of what questions to ask and what information to gather
- Separation of facts from opinions and assumptions
- Making logical and well-thought out decisions
- Developing a formula/method to apply to new situations

I believe that everyone possesses a basic level of critical thinking. We exercise this skill in ways that we may not realize but it is done on a daily basis. Determining what to wear on any given day, deciding on which item to order from the menu at a restaurant, researching which technological gadget we should invest our money in- all of these require the holistic approach of critical thinking. Since we seem to use it for very basic decisions, it is also important that we exercise this skill and use it as a means to become successful. Here are some ways in which you can improve on your critical thinking skills:

1. **Gather information**. It is impossible to make a logical and well-informed decision without knowing all of the facts, or as many as possible. The information we gather cannot simply be focused on one side either. Information gathering should be focused on both the best and worst-case scenarios so we are fully prepared for anything that comes our way. We must know and understand all aspects before making a decision or planning a course of action.

2. **Be open minded and flexible**. We have to understand that part of thinking critically about a matter will involve including facts and information that we may not like or agree with. In addition, after thinking critically, we may realize that the most logical decision may not be what we really want to do (classic conflict between what the brain decides we need and what the heart decides we want). Thinking critically will not always result in a favorable decision but the goal is to make a favorable

outcome that it in your best interest or the best interest of the circumstances presented. This requires flexibility in your thought process.

3. **Question everything**. As children our sense of curiosity was at an all-time high. Everything was new to us so we questioned every aspect of it. This continued through our early stages of education when we were taught the 5 W's (who, what, when, where and why). Somehow this curiosity started to dissipate because the answers could be researched and things began to be accepted for how they appeared to be. Critical thinking is all about finding that curiosity again and asking questions constantly. It allows us to take different perspectives, view matters from different angles, and get to the core of what we need to address.

4. **Map it out**. I am a huge proponent of writing out ideas and flushing them out. This process can be as simple as creating a pros and cons list where you would list all the positive aspects of making a decision in comparison to the negative aspects. This method is particularly beneficial for someone who is a visual person and needs to have information written down and visualized in order to process and make a decision.

PROBLEM SOLVING

While critical thinking plays a role on numerous levels, I want to focus attention to its use addressing problems. The reason why this is important is because we are always going to encounter more problems than solutions on our journey to success. The ability to address these problems is required to excel, especially in a professional environment. Employers are actively seeking candidates that can not only think critically to improve their productivity, but also someone who can identify and address potential or actual problems as they present themselves.

The fundamentals of critical thinking remain relevant when problem solving but there is one key difference- our emotions tend to play a greater role when we are faced with adversity or challenging positions. It is important to rely on reasoning and logic rather than make decisions that are based on emotion. This is easier said than done but problem-solving skills can be developed and strengthened with practice and with having a greater awareness of our feelings and the role they play in decision making. When engaging in critical thinking while problem solving, the following steps are recommended:

1. **Identify the problem**. The first and most important step is in identifying what, if any, problems exist. There is a chance that there is no problem at all and perhaps there was an issue in properly understanding the situation. However, if it appears that there a problem to solve it is important to define and understand what that problem is. The reason this is such an important step is because if you label something as a problem incorrectly you will waste time and energy attempting to fix something that is not broken.

2. **Analyze the problem**. Once the problem has been identified it is important to view it from multiple angles or perspectives to get a better understanding of it. By analyzing the problem you can begin to understand some of its nuances, like how it occurred, whether it can even be solved, and if you are equipped to handle the matter alone or need support. This process can also reveal what role, if any, your emotions play in the process. Remember- critical thinking involves an objective, or unbiased, view.

3. **Explore and research potential solutions**. True power is found in options. There may be more than one way to solve a problem so it is best to research multiple viable solutions. It is better to worry about editing the list after you write down whatever comes to mind. Once you have a list you can begin to select the best options before moving onto the next step.

4. **Evaluate the options and decide on the best one**. There is no guarantee that a potential solution will fix a problem. It is important to understand what the problem truly is while evaluating the potential solution for the best fix. In evaluating you must weigh the benefits and pitfalls that may arise with a potential solution. The potential solution that offers the least concerns, while also addressing the core of the problem, takes you to the final step.

5. **Take action**. Implement your solution to the problem accordingly. Depending on the problem, the solution may take time or may be

immediately addressed. It is important not to abandon the critical thinking component while addressing the problem.

Critical thinking and problem solving go well beyond marketable skills in an educational or employment setting. These skills can increase our confidence level as well as our self-worth.

CHAPTER 6

EMOTIONAL INTELLIGENCE

"As more and more artificial intelligence is entering into the world, more and more emotional intelligence must enter into leadership."
– Amit Ray

One of the growing soft skills sought in the professional world is emotional intelligence. As the name suggests, it is focused on being aware and managing one owns emotions. Included in that, and very relevant in a professional setting, is the need to be aware of and navigate through the emotions of people around you as well. A concept that was introduced in the early 1990's, emotional intelligence has growingly become a must-have in professionals and is credited for achieving great levels of success. It also happens to be a concept that I believe is not widely understood or known.

Emotional intelligence encompasses a set of critical skills that impacts what you do and say on a daily basis. It affects how we manage our behavior, navigate through complex social situations, and guide us as we aim to make decisions that will lead to positive results. Essentially it consists of two major aspects- the personal aspect and the social aspect.

The personal aspect relates to the ability to be self-aware and self-manage your emotions and behaviors. Examples of this include your ability to persevere in difficult situations and how we exercise self-control in challenging situations. The social aspect relates to the relationships we have with other people and how we manage the complexities related to those interactions. Examples of this include your ability to get along with other people and work together on group tasks.

Below are some of the signs of emotional intelligence that have been highlighted numerous times by the professionals I surveyed as being among the most critical:

- **Emotional control** - One of my favorite reminders from a friend is to never make permanent decisions based on temporary emotions. In a professional setting the likelihood of emotions playing a role or becoming relevant, especially when interacting with multiple personalities, is very high. It is critical to think and plan before acting or responding, especially when emotions are involved.

- **Authenticity** - Say what you mean, mean what you say, stand by your principles and values, and do not compromise your individuality. The truth is that everyone is not going to like who you are and that is a part of life. This should not deter you from being genuine and honest about who you are. Those who value authenticity, who will likely be people who matter, will recognize this strength in you.

- **Empathy** - Showing empathy involves understanding other people's feelings and thoughts. It is exercised by placing yourself in the "shoes" of the other person and attempting to understand their position. In doing so you are not

38

as quick to assume or judge a person. You do not have to agree with the other person's position but you can grow a greater understanding of it, which can impact the tone and focus of a conversation.

- **Support others** - A true sign of leadership is when someone is able to encourage and motivate others to become the best version of themselves. As leadership is a valuable commodity in the professional world, you must keep this in mind. Compliment others on their performance. Acknowledge hard work in others. Show appreciation for dedication and applaud achievements. Emotional intelligence is relevant here because this skill involves placing others ahead of yourself. This can be challenging but rewarding for all parties involved.

- **Stay committed** - Character and integrity are invaluable in a professional world. Your ability to stay committed to seeing a task through not only strengthens these qualities but demonstrates a high level of emotional intelligence. It will always be easier to quit, especially when times get difficult or a more interesting distraction presents itself. Consistently staying committed speaks to your reliability and trustworthiness as a professional.

TESTING FOR EMOTIONAL INTELLIGENCE

In a professional setting, assessing emotional intelligence can be done in different manners. This can range from observing your approach to your work, gauging your interactions with your co-workers and supervisor(s), and evaluating how you handle challenging circumstances. However, this is all done once you are on the job. The assessment of emotional intelligence starts well before you even get an offer for employment.

Although Chapter 10 of this book focuses on interview skills, I want to demonstrate how emotional intelligence can be assessed as early as during an entrance interview for employment or related. To gauge the level of emotional intelligence a candidate possesses, responses will be assessed based on their honesty, humility, and the perception the candidate has of what other people think are strengths and weaknesses. Here are some examples of questions that seek to discover your level of emotional intelligence:

1. What motivates you to do your work?
2. How do you motivate others to get their work done?
3. Describe a stressful work situation that you have experienced. How did you handle that?
4. Describe a conflict you had with a supervisor. How did you handle that?
5. Tell me about a time when you received feedback from a supervisor at work that you disagreed with. How did you handle that?
6. How do your colleagues benefit by working with you?
7. What is the most challenging aspect about working in a group setting? How do you overcome that challenge?
8. Who inspires you? Why?

9. How comfortable are you asking for help or support?
10. What would your co-workers at your previous job say about you?

Emotional intelligence has played a tremendous role in my success. I was never academically strong and could not compete with many on this level. I made up for this by constantly developing my emotional intelligence and the skills related. I do not want to undermine the importance of academics; however, academics alone will not make you the most marketable candidate in the professional world. A well-rounded candidate will be the most marketable and emotional intelligence plays a great role in that assessment.

CHAPTER 7

DRESS FOR SUCCESS

"You cannot climb the ladder of success
dressed in the costume of failure."
- Zig Ziglar

The topic of dress and clothing, and my views related to them, has made the greatest impact in my professional life. Growing up when told to put on a dress shirt and slacks, or worse yet a suit, I felt that it was a punishment for something I did wrong. I was uncomfortable, these clothes always made me hot and cranky, and I felt like I could not move freely. I would often look at adults who wore formal clothing daily and wondered how or why they looked so comfortable, and why they would voluntarily choose to wear those clothes. I remember swearing to myself that I would never voluntarily wear a suit, even as an adult, unless I had absolutely no option. Times have changed for me drastically.

The level of excitement I now have in shopping for and wearing my professional clothing is beyond words. I have more professional clothing, ranging from suits, shirts, ties, and dress shoes, than I do "relaxed" clothing (i.e. jeans, t-shirts and sneakers). I carefully select the dress shirt to match the tie, to match the socks, to match the shoes, and tie it all together with the perfect matching watch. I walk out of my front door feeling like I own the world and everything in it. Regardless of how I feel waking up I leave my house dressed professionally with my head held high, confidence on full blast, and a smile on my face.

The power of clothing is indescribable but the effects and benefits are absolutely measurable- in the relationships you make that day, in the responses of people when you approach them, in the looks you get as you walk down the street, and how you personally feel when entering a room.

To be clear, professional attire is not limited to suits, dress shirts, and ties. Various professionals and professional settings call for and hold different expectations. Different settings carry different expectations of what clothing is deemed appropriate and suitable. Sometimes a uniform is ideal and at other times dressing casually may be a necessity. As a lawyer I can only speak specifically about my "uniform" which consists of a suit and related items. I choose to wear the same uniform when visiting schools, doing public speaking engagements, or meeting with actual or potential clients. Regardless of what clothing is expected of you in your professional setting understand that certain fundamental requirements are present nonetheless, as described below.

When discussing the importance of professional attire with young people I have often heard two issues raised. First, it is unfair that we live in a society where people are judged for what they wear and that negative judgments or assumptions may be associated. Second, by wearing a suit to conform to the expectations of society or that particular profession or workplace, it can be viewed as the equivalent of "selling out" and being someone you are not. While I certainly hear and understand these views, it is important to approach them from a different standpoint to address them.

First, while it is absolutely unfair that we judge people based on what they wear sadly that is how society works. While we can aim to advocate for a change in this approach moving forward, we must understand and play by the rules for now. Second, wearing professional clothes is so much more than doing it to appease others. It builds confidence and self-esteem and also commands respect when you enter a room. If conforming is an issue you can absolutely find your own style and bring your personality to light in what you wear. From your shirt, to ties or bow ties, to socks, you can be as unique as you want while also playing the game. You do not need to sacrifice who you are as a person by dressing professionally.

Additional insight and factors about why professional attire plays such a critical role in achieving success include the following-

1. **First impressions are key.** You can only make a first impression once so it is always best to make the greatest impression to start. A person in a suit is received as a person with focus and determination as well as someone who understands the importance of presentation. When you walk away you want people to remember you for all the right reasons and the right professional attire will absolutely be one of those memorable positive factors.

2. **Dress for the position you desire, not the position you hold.** If you want to be a leader, or a boss, or a very important person, you have to dress the part. It is almost like the clothes and the mental state you enter into when dressed

professionally wills the things you want into your grasp. You place yourself into a position where you are dressing for, and prepared to accept, greatness to welcome you.

3. **Keep it clean.** While professional attire can range based on profession, it is critical to keep in mind that certain aspects should be present regardless- it must be neat, clean, matching, and ironed. Whether you are wearing a suit or a uniform, how it fits on you, how it looks, and how clean it comes together are all crucial. I have seen too many lawyers in suits that are dirty, baggy, wrinkled, or mismatched. The quality of the work that you do may be reflected by your presentation.

One key misconception that I have heard, and once held, is that professional clothing (specifically suits) is way too expensive to purchase. Depending on your taste it can absolutely get very expensive. However, the amazing thing about professional clothing is that if you buy the right suit, and wear it the right way, it will look more expensive than what it really is. Unlike with other brand clothing, the brand itself is not on full display to let people know how much you paid for it. The right size and the right fit will have you looking, and feeling, like a million dollars. In addition, most dress shoes or shirts can be purchased for significantly less than most popular sneakers, including Jordans.

The craze to buy expensive brand clothing as opposed to professional clothing is a bad investment. A suit is an investment in your professional life, which ultimately creates greater earning value and potential than a pair of sneakers or jeans. I have found myself investing more in suits, dress shirts, dress shoes, and accessories as my brand continues to grow and my visibility increases. I choose to invest in myself and my brand and I acquire the tools that help me to promote them in the best way possible.

I have heard the advice and suggestions of some people claiming that there needs to be a break in the correlation of suits and the professional world, with those individuals wearing jeans, sweats, and hats claiming that such attire is appropriate. Those individuals, who are arguably well-established in their field, may have more leniency shown to them but young professionals should be wary of such advice. While there are many people who argue to break the cycle of suit-wearing as professional attire, I am a fierce advocate of the power of suits. Beyond the physical, and including the mental, the effects are immeasurable.

As an entrepreneur and lawyer, I cannot begin to describe the positive effects that wearing professional clothing has done for me, ranging from new opportunities and experiences to lasting connections.

CHAPTER 8

THE HANDSHAKE

"Your handshake has the power to reveal your strength of character, make a promise, demonstrate your level of respect, exercise your etiquette, and represent your business acumen. Learning how to do it well will take you far in life and in business."
- Susan C. Young

Arguably one of the most critical nonverbal communication methods in the professional world that can speak volumes about who you are is the handshake. The importance of the handshake goes back many years and has always been symbolic of mutual agreement and respect. The absolute need for both men and women to possess the ability to execute a proper professional handshake is key.

How does a nonverbal action like a handshake carry so much significance? In order to understand this concept you must understand the psychology behind it. The person with whom you are shaking hands with can and will make judgments about your character and personality based on how you deliver a handshake. These judgments from a handshake can range from a sense of confidence, importance, and friendliness to arrogance and overconfidence. Those judgments can also include weakness and insecurity.

The proper handshake at the start or end of an encounter can ultimately set the tone of a meeting or ensure that you will receive a communication following the meeting. A firm handshake, with solid eye contact, and great body language can open doors to opportunities and relationships. The amazing part is that all of this can happen without a single word being said.

I do not want to undermine or overlook the importance of handshakes and greetings in an informal setting, such as meeting friends or family. The value of a handshake can lead to success not just professionally but socially as well. The formality of the handshake or greeting is not as critical informally as it is in a professional setting but it can also provide avenues for growth, developing relationships, and solidifying connections. It is important to evaluate the circumstances and the situation to determine when a more formal or informal greeting is mandated when in a non-professional setting. However, I personally choose to always default to a proper handshake in a professional setting in order to set the right tone.

It is important to also note that a proper handshake applies regardless of gender. I have often heard from men that they are unsure how to handle an encounter with a woman in a professional setting, which often leads to awkward and clumsy introductions. The standard for a proper professional handshake applies to both men and women, while the judgments and assumptions, both positive and negative, also apply.

In delivering a proper handshake there are several key factors that also play a role. First, you must always be prepared to deliver a handshake in a professional setting. That means ensuring that your right hand is always free to shake someone's hand. Transitioning anything from your right hand to your left hand should take place before the opportunity to shake hands to avoid any awkward delays. Second, you must consider your body language. If seated, always stand and face the person with whom you are about to shake hands. Eye contact is incredibly important as it conveys respect as well as a sense of self-confidence. In addition, avoid having your hands in your pockets, as having your hands out and ready to shake demonstrates an invitation to shake hands while also conveying openness and friendliness. Lastly, you must be aware of what your hands are doing both during and after the handshake.

Your hand should be approaching a handshake perpendicular with the goal of making direct and firm contact. Wrap your fingers around the other person's hand as if you were giving their hand a hug. Once contact is made it is customary to squeeze firmly, matching the same level of squeeze as the other person and not squeezing too hard. Pump the shake up and down 2-3 times, shaking from your elbow as opposed to your wrist. Once the hands are released you take a step back. While there is so much to consider in shaking hands it is important to get in a lot of practice so it becomes second nature and you do not have to think or worry about what to do or not do. With enough practice you will start hearing those compliments like "nice handshake", which is always a step in the right direction.

With a greater understanding of the proper handshake, it is also important to understand the types of negative and improper handshakes to avoid delivering along with the messages that these handshakes can send to the person on the receiving end. If you feel your handshake falls into one of these categories, here is an excellent opportunity to work on and practice how to deliver a better handshake. Here is an overview of some of the more popularly recognized improper handshakes that all professionals want to avoid.

The Dead Fish: This handshake, as it sounds, involves a limp, lifeless hand being placed into the hand of someone else with little to no firmness applied along with little to no shake involved. This type of handshake can lead the receiver to believe that you are insecure, lack confidence in yourself, and/or that you are a passive person. From the standpoint of an employer, a potential business contact, or even someone you want to network with, these messages are all wrong and give the receiver hesitation and doubts about what you bring to the table.

The Hand Crusher: This handshake is by far my least favorite and it incorporates two types of handshakes: (1) the one where the person does everything right in the approach and contact but the squeeze is over the top; or (2) the one where the person starts the squeeze before the proper contact is made and ends up grabbing your fingers as opposed to your palm. Some people believe that a hard squeeze sends a powerful, positive message. Unfortunately, it does not. The firmness of your handshake should match, and not exceed, the receiver's firmness. Sometimes this extra use of force is due to a person not knowing their own strength but can easily be addressed with practice. The receiver of this handshake is likely to assume that you are exerting some form of dominance or intimidation.

The Dominator: This handshake can also send the message of dominance without the extra use of force as described above. This involves more of the approach to the actual handshake. As mentioned previously, the proper way to approach a handshake is perpendicular. A change in the approach can send the wrong signal. If approaching with the palm facing up, it sends the message of passiveness or submission. If approaching with the palm facing down, it sends the message of dominance or that the person has the upper hand in the encounter. A perpendicular approach conveys equal ground and mutual respect.

The Queen: If you have ever seen high royalty "shake hands", you will notice that it does not follow any of the rules above. Instead of a meeting of palms it is more of a meeting of fingers, as one person, usually the higher-ranking person, places their fingers onto the submissive hands of the other person. In a professional setting, I have experienced this more times than I care to admit. I often joke when discussing this handshake how I feel a sense of confusion about whether to kiss the hand or not. Typically this type of handshake hints at a desire to maintain personal space. Although the assumption that the perpetrator of this handshake is primarily women, there are plenty of men who engage in a similar approach to handshakes.

The Sweaty Hand: This type of handshake is personally the most frustrating of the group for two reasons. First, it is something that I often have to deal with, as my hands can get sweaty at times. And second, this type of handshake is the only one you can't really practice to avoid. It tends to happen in situations where we get nervous or anxious. While the only advice to give to someone with sweaty palms is to inconspicuously try to wipe them before a handshake, my advice is more for the recipient. It is important to note that sweaty palms are involuntary and not a sign of a lack of respect or professionalism. It is important to maintain your professionalism under these circumstances and not make comments or facial expressions to demonstrate discomfort. This will only make the situation more awkward and could potentially hurt the person who has to endure this involuntary situation.

It's interesting to think that an entire chapter in a book can be devoted to what people may simply believe is a handshake that carries little to no significance. The handshake is one of the tools that you must keep sharp and ready in your arsenal to give you an advantage and an edge in your professional pursuits. And as with all skills we wish to sharpen and master, practice makes perfect.

CHAPTER 9

APPEARANCE & FIRST IMPRESSION

"You never get a second chance to make
a first impression"
- Will Rogers.

A first impression encompasses many aspects. Thus far I have mentioned the non-verbal aspects, which include dress and the professional handshake. By preparing correctly you can lay a solid foundation where the person(s) you are greeting have made some type of positive assumption about who you are. Now comes the hard part- confirming their positive assumptions verbally. This part involves opening and engaging in conversation that is meaningful and is purpose driven.

Before we engage in a conversation we must set up a mental game plan. This is done by asking yourself a few questions:

- Who is the person you seek to converse with?
- What do you believe they ultimately want from the conversation?
- What do you ultimately want from the conversation?

In understanding the importance of these questions, as well as the responses, you are placed in a better position to both initiate a conversation as well as drive the conversation in the direction that benefits both parties involved. In the event that you do not have a clearly defined purpose the goal should be to get a business card or contact information at a minimum. If you walk away from a conversation having gained nothing, offered nothing, and having no way to follow-up, then you likely missed out on an opportunity.

In your moment of truth, your mental approach is set, you look sharp, and you are prepared to deliver the ultimate of professional handshakes. Everything works and now you are about to engage in a conversation with another person. What do you do? What do you say? What do you avoid doing? It is very difficult to focus on so much when engaging in a conversation while worrying about making a positive first impression and also avoiding any pitfalls or mistakes. With practice, the process becomes very fluid and requires little thought. However, it is important to focus on several key elements when engaging in a conversation to ensure that you make a positive first impression that resonates with the other person long after you have left.

- **Remember the key details**. When you meet someone the start of the conversation usually involves an exchange of general information. This generally includes the person's name, a brief description of who they are and/or what they do, and maybe some detail about why the person is there. It is important to keep a mental note of this information and to repeat certain details during the conversation. This shows you were paying attention to the person when they were speaking (and enhances your favorable impression being made).

- **Show interest in the person and conversation**. As you meet professionals in various capacities you will discover one unifying thing- they love to talk about themselves. It is difficult when you want to share your story and purpose while listening to the other person share their story. Be patient, don't rush the conversation, and show interest in what is being said. If it becomes too overwhelming, or you spend the whole time listening and can't get a word out, see below on how to exit a conversation professionally.

- **Have a few backup plans**. At times in a conversation the momentum can slow down. This can become particularly frustrating when you still have a purpose you are trying to achieve. Always have a few conversation starters or topics handy in situations like this. Try to avoid generic questions or topics that have likely been used overused, such as "What brings you here?" or "What is your story?". You also want to avoid interrogating the person by asking questions that are too personal. Instead, offer more thought provoking questions such as "How does your work tie in with your passion?" or "What is the highlight of your daily routine?". I remember a student asking me after a workshop "What would you do if money was not an issue?". I loved the question and at the same time really had to think to answer it because I was never asked that before.

- **Always maintain eye contact**. Establishing and maintaining eye contact sends a positive message that you are paying attention and makes the person you are speaking with feel important and special. In addition, maintaining eye contact helps us to focus on what is being said so we can better retain the information. It is important, however, to be mindful of our eye contact as well. It is important to take breaks from direct eye contact to avoid feelings of aggression or awkwardness. Looking away here and there is important, provided you are not looking away to something inappropriate such as your watch or the next person you want to talk to.

- **Be confident in your body language**. As if focusing on what you need to say and avoid saying is not enough, you also have to manage your body and the messages that it sends as well. Certain behaviors such as swaying back and forth, playing with your hair (this includes facial hair for men), and slouching all send negative messages that can make the other person feel uncomfortable or anxious. Those signals will likely lead them to end the conversation sooner than you would like. You should stand straight, keep your hands at your sides or use them in controlled and meaningful ways, and make sure you are facing the other person speaking. Saying the right thing and carrying yourself the right way will keep a conversation going.

- **Exit plan ready**. Ending a conversation can be desired for several reasons. From a negative standpoint, you may feel the conversation is dragging or lacks purpose. From a positive standpoint, you may feel the conversation hit its marks and it is time to work the room and focus on your next target. It could simply be that you have to make a call or use the bathroom. Regardless of the situation you have to aim to end the conversation respectfully and professionally as opposed to just walking away or visibly letting your interest wane. Remember, all exits should be accompanied by a professional handshake as well. There are different methods of ending the conversation but the three I can honestly say I use more than any other are:

1. "It's been great meeting you. Enjoy the rest of your day/evening." – sometimes being absolutely direct and honest works best.

2. "Can I have your business card so I can follow-up with you?" OR "Here is my card- feel free to reach out to me." – exchanging information usually is an indication that the conversation is ending.

3. "Please excuse me, I have to…" – if something comes up and you have to excuse yourself, be honest and excuse yourself. Just make sure that you do what you are being excused for so it doesn't look like you just wanted to escape the conversation. Also, keep the excuse professional and not personal.

As a professional I have met countless numbers of other professionals or students through my work. It is incredibly difficult to remember everyone but I absolutely remember those who stood out for all the right reasons. Knowing this, I make sure that I am fully prepared when meeting new professionals. My goal is to stand out and be remembered while avoiding the risk of being a nameless, faceless memory. A positive first impression can do wonders in ensuring that you are remembered. Even better, it can help to ensure that there will be an opportunity to make a second impression.

CHAPTER 10

INTERVIEW SKILLS

"Take risks: if you win, you will be happy;
if you lose, you will be wise."
- Author Unknown

The job interview- three words that either bring absolute terror and fear to some or excitement and promise to others. Either way, a job interview is a necessary aspect of the professional world. An interview can take many shapes and forms, ranging from one-on-one interviews to group interviews, or can be a formal interview in an office or an informal interview in a coffee shop. Regardless of the circumstances, the approach leading to an interview as well as the plan of action during the interview will ultimately play a large role in determining if you are asked back for another interview or even offered a position.

For the sake of time and space I am going to assume you have applied for, and been granted, an opportunity to interview for a position that is of interest to you. Congratulations! Before you reach the actual interview there is a lot of homework which must be done.

Part of that homework involves packaging who you are and what you offer to any employer or company. This package includes your resume (which we will discuss later in the book), a cover letter (if applicable), and a list of reliable and positive references from people who can speak to your work ethic and professionalism. In addition to this tangible package, you should also be prepared to justify why you are qualified for the position, why the employer should consider your application, and what makes you different from the numerous other qualified people who have also likely applied for the same position.

The next aspect of your homework involves research into the company you are seeking employment from. Understand the job posting and the position that the company is seeking to fill, including the responsibilities and qualifications, both technically as well as the soft skills (team leader, communication, organization, etc.). Research the company and understand the work they do, what the mission statement is, the changes the company has made over the years to reinforce its mission, and the role of its employees within the company.

If you are lucky enough to know who will be interviewing you, do research on that person too. Find out what their position is in the company, how long he/she has been in the company, and any background information on their path prior to reaching their current position. All of this information not only serves as conversation points but also helps you to best frame your approach and the message you want to deliver during the interview.

With your homework completed, it is now time to confidently walk into a job interview. As with all other professional meetings the interview should start with a firm professional handshake. Take note of the name or names of your interviewer(s) and use it during the interview, as this shows respect and an attention to detail on key aspects. Eye contact is key. If there is more than one interviewer it is important to work the room with your eyes, focusing on the person asking you the question initially then making eye contact with all of the interviewers when responding to a question. Keep your responses clear and concise. Make sure to answer the question asked while not being redundant or going off on a random tangent about something outside of the scope of the question. Avoid being robotic during the interview in your responses or body language. It is important to be loose and relaxed while also being mindful of the setting and its importance. Personally, I like to infuse a bit of humor into a job interview. Partly because I like to joke around but also, as a former employer doing interviews, it can get very boring and repetitive. A break in the monotony with some humor is refreshing. Lastly, be honest. Do not make up stories or experiences because you not only risk getting caught in a lie but you do not want to sell yourself on something that you are not able to back-up if the opportunity presents itself down the line.

When researching information to support the themes in my book, I spoke with a few professionals who suggested some really interesting approaches to an interview. One professional suggested appealing to the five senses of the interviewer. Professional clothes (sight), a confident and projected voice (hearing), a nice and friendly smell that is not overwhelming (smell), leaving a lasting impression following your interview (loosely interpreted as taste), and a solid opening and closing professional handshake (touch) are all key elements.

Another professional spoke about the tone of the interviewee during the interview. He suggested that the person speak as though you already have the job and it's just a matter of when you will start. While obviously avoiding any sense of arrogance, this level of confidence shows an interviewer that you believe in yourself and showcases what you bring to the position. I love both approaches but ultimately it is up to you to determine what method best works for you, based on the circumstances.

A large part of interviewing is the ability to respond to questions on the spot related to your skills as well as your personality and character. Interviewers have become increasingly savvy when it comes to formulating these questions, as they can take many forms and not seem like a professional question when it is in fact one. Many of these questions are psychologically based and reveal aspects about who you are, sometimes without you even realizing it.

As I developed my research for this book, I wanted to get a first-hand experience of some of the more unique questions being asked in interviews. I decided to not only ask employers but to also go on several interviews and note the questions being asked. Here are some of the more interesting questions asked during interviews and some insight into how to respond:

- What are your greatest strengths and weaknesses? The knee-jerk response is to list a laundry list of amazing strengths and say you have no weaknesses. Please do not do this. In listing your strengths, be humble. Focus on the strengths that are relevant to the position you are interviewing for. In considering any weaknesses be mindful of avoiding an example that will ultimately hurt you (like the time someone told me during an interview that their greatest weakness was waking up on time). Instead, find a weakness that hints at a positive. For example, saying that you feel you invest too much of yourself in your work seems like a negative but also hints that you are passionate and dedicated.

- <u>Where do you see yourself in 5 years?</u> Some people may think that saying something to the effect of "working with this company and for you" is the clever response. The truth is that an employer that asks this is really testing your level of ambition and ability to think ahead in your plan for success. If you really envision being with the company state that you envision yourself at a higher position doing greater work and having more influence. Please avoid saying "I don't know", even if that is the case, as it places your ambition level into question, which is never good during an interview.

- <u>Why are you leaving your current position?</u> In the situation where you are leaving a current position and interviewing for a new one, an employer will definitely want to know why you are transitioning. This is not an opportunity to bad-mouth your current employer or employees, or complain about your salary, or speak negatively about anything that may come off as being minor. The safest response is in saying you feel you want to grow or that you have outgrown your current position. Be honest in the response but also evaluate the potential damage that it can cause and adjust accordingly.

- What are your salary requirements/expectations? While there are different takes on how to respond to this question, I will offer my two cents to the conversation. It is important for you to understand your worth as an employee and ensure that your employer not only recognizes your worth but compensates you for it. Don't be afraid to request a salary you feel you deserve, obviously within reason, and also stress that sometimes the salary is not the only way an employee can be compensated (vacation days, schedule flexibility, etc.).

- If you were an animal, which animal would you be and why? This is one of the trickier questions that has interviewees underestimating its importance. This is very much a psychological question and arguably one of my favorite to ask. Ultimately, this question is asking you to select an animal that demonstrates or possesses the characteristics that not only link to you but also are desirable for an employer to have in an employee. So, saying you are like an elephant because you have a good memory or like a cheetah because you are fast would not apply here. Do not be fooled by the informality of this question and use it to solidify your eligibility for the position.

- Do you have any questions for us? It breaks my heart when a person is asked this and they respond by saying they have no questions. Even if you don't have any questions- ask a question. You can ask details on the position or the expectations, ask about the interviewer (remember professionals love to talk about themselves), or if all else fails ask about the hiring process in terms of timing or rounds. Avoid asking questions about how many vacation days you get, or the policy on latenesses, or how soon before you get a raise (all of which I have been asked at some point). This is your opportunity to turn the tables and ask questions which shows an interest in your part in the position. Please do not waste this opportunity.

The journey is not over after the interview. You still have an opportunity to make a positive impression on the interviewer. Always send a thank you e-mail after you have interviewed. Keep in mind this will require having the contact information as well as the name of the person or persons who interviewed you. In this outreach take the opportunity to re-establish your interest in the position. If you are told that the process of making a decision could take two weeks do not reach out multiple times in that period asking if a decision was made. You want to show interest and eagerness but you do not want to cross the line and make things awkward or uncomfortable. Lastly, keep interviewing. Never put all of your eggs in one basket and waste valuable time waiting to hear from one position. The companies are not doing it so why should you?

Although the location, format, or style of an interview can vary based on the professional setting, the work required to adequately prepare remains the same. Up until this point you have made enough of an impression with your resume to warrant a deeper look into who you are. The interview sets the stage to not only showcase your value as a person but also an opportunity for you to advocate for an opportunity to showcase your skills in a professional setting.

Remember that you will likely be one of many who will interview for a position. You can separate yourself from the pack with the proper preparation, presentation and determination.

CHAPTER 11

NETWORKING

"Networking is marketing. Marketing yourself,
marketing your uniqueness,
marketing what you stand for."
- Christine Comaford-Lynch

As mentioned previously, the mentality necessary to be successful in life requires an approach similar to playing chess as opposed to playing checkers. I believe there is nowhere else where this is most prevalent than in networking. The level of planning, strategy, anticipation, reaction, and response in chess is mirrored when navigating through the professional world. Meeting and greeting individuals who may possess an opportunity or connection that could help you achieve a greater level of success requires a methodical and calculated approach. Networking is a skill that must be respected, worked on regularly to be mastered, and is absolutely necessary for any professional.

Unfortunately, as the importance of networking continues to grow the ability and skill set of many people to network, particularly young professionals and primarily due to the tremendous rise and reliance on social media, is declining. On the flip side, many young professionals are finding innovative and unique ways to network and brand themselves using social media. It is important for young professionals to understand and value the power of networking as well as the right and wrong ways to do so. For starters, it is important to understand what the goals of networking are. Networking is done to make contacts; to develop relationships; to discover or create new opportunities; to create professional allies and/or potential mentors; to showcase your skills and your brand; and so many other reasons. Whatever your reasons are for wanting to network it is important to understand how to effectively do so as well as what pitfalls to avoid.

Prior to placing yourself into a networking environment one of the first important tools to have ready in your arsenal is your elevator pitch. An elevator pitch is a brief persuasive speech that you use to market yourself, your business, and/or your company. It should be succinct, memorable and unique. While the timing of the pitch, for more skilled professionals, should be around 30 seconds, I recommend young professionals aim for anywhere between 60-90 seconds. The reason being that a young professional, who may lack extensive experience, will need to advocate harder for an opportunity.

In formulating your elevator pitch you must think of what the goal is for the pitch. This may change based on the scenario but it is good to have a handy one-size-fits-all pitch. You must then explain what it is that you do and what is it that you offer that is unique and fits the need of the listener. As you close out your pitch you need to have a goal in mind. If it is to continue to engage in conversation have a question ready that leads to dialogue. If the goal is collect a business card then ask for a card and exchange your business card, which you should have and be ready to share. As with all things, practice makes perfect.

In order to become effective at networking, and to also build your network, you have to throw yourself into social events and put into practice your skills. This can be frightening for some people as you may be entering a social event where you don't know anything and have to talk to strangers. Honestly, with the exception of the few who do know others, a majority of people at these events are in the same place as you.

If you do not feel comfortable being alone then go with a networking partner. Not someone who wants to just hang out but someone like-minded and in the pursuit of developing their networking skills. I remember an awesome period of my life following law school where a close friend of mine and I went to random social events and just worked the room, speaking to people and collecting business cards and insight. While we made a fun night out of it, on a professional level it was truly empowering.

When "working the room" at an event, there are some key things to keep in mind. Your approach and movement must be calculated and focused, even when having a good time and challenging yourself.

- **Bring your business cards with you and have them ready to distribute**. At a social event a person is not going to remember your name or e-mail at the end of the night. You want them to walk away with a means of contacting you, and vice versa.

- **Dress to impress**. Neat, clean, and professional is key. Your attire will attract people to you, as you will look like you are a VIP.

- **Manage your time**. Avoid wasting precious moments spending time with people you already know. Move around and meet new people. Try to avoid spending too much time in one conversation, especially if that conversation is not worth your time. Just as important, do not waste other people's time either. You are not the only one aiming to work the room so don't tie people up.

- **Be the problem solver**. When approaching people think about and present what you can offer as opposed to what you need or want. Aim to establish a win-win situation for all parties involved, including yourself. This can be incorporated in your elevator pitch.

While there are many positives of networking, and the goal is to enjoy as much of those positive rewards and relationships that can potentially come from it, it is important to network with the mindset that you should not expect anything from anyone. If your goal is to constantly hunt for the next person that will help you, or to fake your way into someone's good graces, you will come off immediately as lacking sincerity.

Connecting with people is not about trying to get something or asking for a favor. Professional contacts can serve as mentors, as advisors, as sounding boards, or can even present you with additional connections. If a connection doesn't result in you getting the job you want or more money in your pocket, it does not mean that it was not worth developing. It is always good to know the right people in the right places because in life you just never know what will happen.

Following a networking event, the goal is to cultivate relationships with people. As with personal relationships, after meeting someone for the first time you should not ask to move in together or propose marriage. In a professional setting the equivalent would be to ask for a job or a letter of recommendation from someone you just met. Developing a relationship entails staying in touch, sharing your progress, asking how the other person is doing and what projects they are working on, and ultimately building trust.

Avoid constantly reaching out as this can be an annoyance. Do not reach out only when you need something. When reaching out by e-mail, keep the e-mail short and to the point, make the e-mail relevant and interesting, and do not make it all about you. Connections on social media such as LinkedIn can be constructive and lead to establishing other connections with people in similar circles.

Networking is a powerful tool that can open doors and create opportunities simply by putting yourself out there and meeting people. While these practices have been outlined assuming you are at a networking event it is important to note that networking can take place anywhere. I have connected personally and professionally with people at the grocery store, the car wash, the laundromat, and even at my son's soccer class. Rather than focus on getting ready for networking opportunities it is important to stay ready, as you never know when you will need that elevator pitch.

CHAPTER 12

RESUME DEVELOPMENT

"Some people dream of success…
while others wake up and work hard at it."
- Author Unknown

The job application process can be very daunting for people. The search for positions can be overwhelming, whether you are looking for a job within a certain type of field or just any job that will hire you. No matter how deserving you are of a position, or how badly you need that opportunity, the ultimate gatekeeper that determines if you can get your foot in the door or not is your resume. A well-crafted resume will impress people, standing out from the countless other resumes submitted, and afford you an opportunity to bring your skills, education, and experiences to life with an in-person interview.

While I will focus primarily on resume development for the purpose of employment, keep in mind that a similar approach should be considered if applying to schools, internships, or volunteer opportunities. Unlike with some other professional approaches or techniques, there are some steadfast rules and guidelines, with few exceptions, for resumes and resume development which I will present.

In resume development I have encountered several ranges in the spectrum. I have encountered people who feel they have way too much information and experiences to fit neatly and succinctly in a resume. I have encountered people, particularly younger or pre-professionals who feel they don't have anything to put into a resume format. And then there is a wide array of in-between, from not knowing the rules of resume development to those who can draft resumes in their sleep.

The easier group to support are those with more information than they know what to do with, as the problem is editing as opposed to figuring out what to put. For younger or pre-professionals, the challenge is in finding meaningful information to put into a resume. I will make sure to offer my two cents on how to work on this area. Regardless of where you fall in the spectrum, I am hoping this chapter will present something new to many and offer advice that is meaningful and useful. I am also hoping that my experience reviewing hundreds of resumes will actually come in handy.

Your resume is a snapshot of who you are as a person as well as what you offer to a potential employer. In thinking about what to include in your resume, or even if you are concerned about what to include if you feel you lack certain experiences, it is important to keep in mind the key characteristics that employers want in an employee. Communication skills, positive attitude, teamwork, willingness to learn, critical thinking skills, self-management, resilience- all of these are key elements in an indispensable employee, or a potential student. These skills can be showcased in the form of employment or through community service, participation in a club or team, or in other meaningful extracurricular activities.

Something that may seem "useless" can be crafted to fit into one or more of the essential skills listed above. It takes careful consideration and thought to craft a job responsibility or extracurricular activity into a desirable professional skill. If you feel you want or need more to add to your resume, then put the work in and make it happen. Your resume will constantly be shifting, changing, and growing as you grow.

Below are a few ways in which you can develop a very solid resume that will not only separate you from the pack but will impress anyone reading it.

1. **Tailor your resume for the position you are applying for**. A one-size-fits-all approach to a resume will not stand out when applying for your desired position. Based on the opportunity you are seeking the employer may require certain skills and experiences. You should tailor your resume to showcase the skills and experience that they are looking for. As a guide use the job posting to highlight what you should focus on in your resume.

2. **Choose your words wisely.** As one tasked to review dozens and dozens of resumes to select potential interviews, I can honestly say that I could not and did not take the time to read each word on each resume. Instead I scanned the resume to look for key words that sparked a reaction. Focus on key words within that particular industry, again utilizing the job posting as a guide. Less is more and the right words will grab the attention of the reader and have them take a closer look at who you are.

3. **Show and prove**. I have seen too many resumes where under the "skills" section people just list a bunch of buzz words and think that the list alone will spark interest. It never worked for me. Showcase the skills you offer by describing how you put them into practice and the positive results of it. For example, if leadership skills are simply placed on the resume with nothing more I will lose interest. However, if you state that you served as a team leader and increased productivity or lead your team to a big win, that will be viewed as impressive and warrants a further look into who you are as a person.

4. **Use a professional format**. While the goal is to stand out, it should be for the skills that you possess and can offer as opposed to how stylish or colorful your resume is. Keep the formatting professional and organized. There are tons of examples of professional formats for a resume so do your research before you finalize your resume.

5. **Tell a story**. The story that you want to share with any potential employer is one of your personal and professional growth. This is shown through your education, experiences, accomplishments, skills and knowledge. Since you do not have the space, and the reader does not have the time, for a long, drawn out story, make sure your story is precise and highlights the benchmarks you have achieved.

6. **One page or not?** I have heard so many contradicting views about whether a resume

should fit neatly into one page or not. I have seen people stretch margins and fonts to their absolute limits to fit a resume on one sheet, which can be overwhelming and unprofessional. Here is my take on the one-page rule. If you are more established and have significant experiences and related to share, having more than one page makes sense. If you are not as established or are in the process of developing a professional presence, you should stick to one page. Ultimately, the goal is to edit any information that is not needed, relevant, or applicable and see where you stand when the smoke clears. Knowing employers skim resumes due to time restraints, if you decide to go longer than one page make sure the information you are presenting is on point.

7. **Proofread. Then do it again. And again**. This will be listed in both the do's and don'ts as it is that important. The quickest way to get your resume tossed is to have grammatical errors and typos. If all an employer has to piece together who you are as a person includes errors, you are making the wrong kind of impression.

While many people follow the proper professional formatting for resume development, there are those who seem to want to follow their own rules. As an employer, I have encountered too many cringe-worthy, disappointing, disheartening and comical aspects of resumes that left me scratching my head wondering what went wrong. Below are the more common pitfalls of resume development as well as in the submission or resumes to interviewers.

1. **Including irrelevant experiences, hobbies, or interests.** With limited space the goal has to be to keep things focused and to highlight what the employer wants to see. With that said, including experiences, hobbies, or interests that are not related, or demonstrate no tangible or relatable skills, is not a good use of space. If it is on your resume, you need to demonstrate how or why it is relevant to the employer. If you cannot, then remove it.

2. **Excessive use of buzz words or jargon.** Terms such as "go-getter," "think outside the box," "team-player" and "people person" are overused and very generic. Try to avoid using catchy terms and use your own words to describe your skill set.

3. **Long paragraphs instead of bullet points.** A resume is not an opportunity to write a novel about your life and experiences. You must keep the reader in mind and assume that time is of the essence. Organize the important and relevant information in a bullet format that makes it easy to transition from skill to skill, point to point. If an employer has to read a paragraph to figure out what to gain from it you are likely to lose their interest.

4. **Don't lie.** The natural inclination is to want to make yourself as marketable and appealing as possible. This can result in including information about yourself, your skills, or your experience that is not accurate. This is a dangerous game to

play and one that can have consequences, even if you are able to get by initially. At some point the skills you claim to possess will be put to the test and there will be no hiding at that point.

5. **Be mindful of the use of tense (past and present).** Misuse of tense was one of the most frequent issues that I encountered in reviewing resumes. Any experiences or employment that took place in the past should be described in the past tense. Anything that is ongoing should be described in the present tense.

6. **Short-term employment.** With some exceptions such as short-term contracts or summer employment, it is important to avoid listing employment that you held for a short period. This includes any employment in which you were fired. This sends negative messages to an employer about your level of commitment as well as your work ethic.

7. **Using an inappropriate e-mail address to submit resumes**. When I mentioned comical earlier to describe the resume review process, this is exactly what I was referring to. The types of e-mail addresses in which resumes were submitted go well beyond professional and into the world of crude and shocking. I would share some of my favorites but this book is rated PG and I want to keep it that way. At the end of the day, you can keep any e-mail you wish but you should absolutely create a professional e-mail that you use for professional communication.

Can't think of one? Just use some formula of your first and last name and you will be set.

Resume development is something that requires time, energy, and attention considering its incredible value. If you really want a position, if you really need a position, then use that energy in getting in the front door by drafting the ideal professional resume.

CHAPTER 13

PUBLIC SPEAKING

"The worst speech you'll ever give, will be far better
than the one you never give."
- Fred Miller

Arguably one of the most dreaded forms of communication is public speaking. Glossophobia, as it is technically referred to as, is the fear of public speaking. The idea of public speaking as a young person was truly terrifying. I would do anything and everything to avoid being called by the teacher or having to present in front of the classroom. I was often so silent that my intentions of becoming a lawyer would be questioned by counselors. After a very focused effort to work on this weakness and identify the root of the issues surrounding it things began to change. I transitioned from fearing any type of public speaking to seeking opportunities to speak. Much of my career today focuses on public speaking, ranging from small events to graduations. Funny enough, I now teach public speaking on a college-level. It was a difficult and challenging growth process but one that I appreciate and value considering its importance in the professional world.

Regardless of the profession you choose to enter there is a likelihood that you will need to do some type of public presentation. You may be called to persuade an audience, motivate an audience to complete a task or achieve a benchmark, or to inform an audience on a particular subject. It also serves as an amazing opportunity to demonstrate leadership skills. An effective leader can communicate with intent, present a clear and concise message, motivate the audience, and address the opinions and concerns of the audience. It is important to understand the skills required to effectively deliver your message regardless of what role you intend on playing.

The art of public speaking is not just limited to the actual public presentation. There is a lot of behind-the-scenes work that goes into making a presentation effective and impactful. The speaker must do an analysis of the audience and plan out speaking goals, determine the best methods on how to engage the audience, and assess how to successfully deliver the chosen message. This requires critical thinking skills as well as the ability to understand and manage both verbal and non-verbal cues. Public speaking requires so much more than just standing in front of an audience. The skills required are transferable to numerous aspects of a well-rounded and marketable professional.

One of the negative aspects of public speaking that needs to be recognized and embraced is nervousness. Even the most experienced public speaker experiences some level of nervousness. The mistake that many people make is that they attribute this sense of nervousness with a feeling of being unprepared or of a pending poor performance. This fear can cause people to run away from public speaking opportunities. In reality, nerves can be a good thing. The rush of adrenaline that accompanies nervousness can increase alertness and focus.

Considering that nervousness is part of the process, it is necessary to expect it and find ways to constructively deal with it. One of the best ways to tackle nervousness before it gets out of hand is to spend a substantial amount of time preparing and practicing. This process, over time, will increase your confidence level and ultimately reduce the nerves. Keep in mind that the feeling of nervousness will always be there but your ability to manage it will strengthen in time.

Here are a few tips that will help in terms of public speaking:

- **Know your audience.** It is important to understand who the message you seek to deliver is intended for. This will assist in crafting the best method to deliver that message. Anticipate what you believe the audience wants to hear and what will carry the strongest impact and craft your presentation accordingly.

- **Organization is key.** A presentation should flow and be organized in an effort to keep the audience engaged and interested. This includes presenting a clear topic, general purpose, specific purpose, central idea, main points and supporting information. A powerful and attention-grabbing introduction sends a strong message to start and should be accompanied by a concise and thought-provoking conclusion.

- **Let your personality shine.** The most unique aspect of a public presentation is the presenter. There is no need to lose your personality in the process. Being genuine will be well-received in comparison to a monotonous presentation which runs the risk of losing the audiences interest. Don't be afraid to infuse humor or a personal story if it is relevant and will grab your audience's attention.

- **Be mindful of your mannerisms.** There are several distracting mannerisms that the presenter should be mindful of and attempt to avoid. Some of these include: clenching or wringing your hands, pacing back and forth, keeping your hands in pockets, jingling change or keys, adjusting your hair or clothing, fidgeting with a pen or marker, placing your arms behind your back, and/or touching your face. As some of these mannerisms may be a subconscious nervous tic it is important to practice your presentation in front of someone or have your presentation recorded and reviewed prior to the real deal.

- **Use an Outline.** Reading from a lengthy script can have several adverse effects. It can limit your eye contact, reduce the projection of your voice, and/or create a disconnect between the presenter and the audience. An outline presents only the key points which serve as reminders of what to discuss. With less to read, the speaker is able to maintain better eye contact which establishes a stronger relationship with the audience.

- **Be wise about using audiovisual aids.** Presenters often like to use audiovisual aids to liven up a presentation. This presents creative ways to convey information and engage the audience. It can, however, open the door to several potential pitfalls. You want to ensure that your audience is focused on you and what you are saying as opposed to reading information off of a Powerpoint slide. In addition, a visual aid opens the door for criticism- visible grammatical errors or issues with the equipment can result in negative reactions. As with all things, make sure to practice prior to presenting.

- **Envision a successful speech.** Part of my routine before delivering any presentation is to clothes my eyes and breath. With my eyes closed I envision myself giving a powerful and dynamic presentation. I envision the positive responses from the audience as well as the empowering feelings that accompany such a response. Once I open my eyes I am excited to make my vision a reality. Avoid any negative thoughts at all costs.

As fearful as you have made public speaking in your head and heart the time has come to tackle your fear head on. Public speaking will play a role in your professional world in one capacity or another. It can be the determining factor in major personal and professional growth. The more you put yourself in positions to speak publicly, the greater the level of comfort and confidence you will develop. You got this!

CHAPTER 14

CONFLICT RESOLUTION

"There are three ways of dealing with difference: domination, compromise, and integration. By domination only one side gets what it wants; by compromise neither side gets what it wants; by integration we find a way by which both sides may get what they wish."
- Mary Parker Follett

People handle conflict in their own way, likely based on their personality and previous experiences. Some people choose to ignore and avoid, others choose to address conflict head on in an effort to resolve, and others revert to various forms of negative options such as name-calling or physical altercation. In a professional setting, many of these methods will not be productive, effective, or even tolerated. Running from a conflict in a professional setting will be just as ineffective as yelling or screaming. Unresolved or ignored conflicts can fester and grow into monsters, at which point resolving it is substantially more difficult. The challenging question is what is the best way to handle conflicts in a professional setting without compromising your character, integrity, or your employment?

A professional setting is a breeding ground for conflict and thus making it unavoidable. This conflict can lead to a lack of productivity, creativity, or the creation of barriers among people who must work together. Why is it the case that conflict is so prevalent in a professional setting? Opposing positions, competitive nature of employees and employers, jealousy, ego, pride, lack of appreciation or compensation, or maybe something as simple as having a bad day can all contribute to conflict. Regardless of what role you play in a professional setting attempting to balance all of these potential factors in an effort to maintain a conflict-free environment seems an insurmountable task. Instead, it might be more productive to focus on the two key areas that lead to a great deal of conflict- communication and emotions.

Communication is often stated as one of, if not the, most essential ingredient to any healthy and positive relationship. This mentality applies in a professional setting. Many professional settings are set up in a way where one person tells another person to tell another person about something that needs to be done. This leads to either poor communication, a lack of communication, or miscommunication. Naturally, conflict can arise in these situations. The goal is to avoid areas of interpretation and assumption when in reality there is none. The ability to clearly, concisely, and accurately communicate with employers, employees, and co-workers can greatly reduce conflict and lead to healthier relationships.

Emotion can also play a negative role in escalating, as opposed to resolving, conflict. Human beings are naturally emotional beings so it is understandable how or why emotions play a role in escalating conflict. In my experience, emotions play a role when we interpret, allow, or drive conflict from professional to personal. We open the door for emotions to creep in once we lose focus of our role in that setting. You must remember that you are there to do a job and all things must fall in line with that premise. You are not employed to make friends, or develop personal relationships, or find your soulmate. If any of that happens coincidentally then that's great. However, that is not your goal or function in that professional setting. Part of playing your position involves identifying and checking emotions that can influence or incite negative behavior. In addition, the ability to empathize, meaning take the position of someone else to understand their thoughts and feelings, is also important in influencing our own emotions and reactions during conflict.

We are all different, with different morals, ideals, beliefs, triggers and responses. It is what makes life interesting and challenging at the same time. In a workplace, this can produce creative and exciting environments or can lead to numerous conflicts and issues. Keeping in mind that no workplace is the same, as no person is the same, it is still possible to identify universal rules for how to handle workplace conflict. Below are some best practices and can and should be applied based on the situation.

-   **Keep in mind the end game.** When engaged in a workplace conflict, you cannot approach it with an "I must win" mentality. Focused solely on getting the upper hand will only lead to more conflict. You should approach conflict with an open and positive mentality with the ultimate goal of seeking a "win-win" situation for everyone involved. While this may not be feasible in every situation, you want to avoid anyone feeling like they lost or have nothing to gain. This could plant a seed for future animosity or conflict.

- **Cooler heads prevail.** Attempting to resolve a conflict when the parties involved are upset or have shut down will not be effective. It is best to allow the parties involved, to take a step back and calm down. This will allow the parties to think rationally and reduce as much of the emotional component as possible.

- **Clearly identify and define the issue.** Sometimes there is conflict when there does not need to be. An argument can arise out of a lack of communication where ultimately all parties involved may be on the same side. It is important to identify what is, if any, the specific issue as well as the opposing sides to the issue. Once this is clearly defined then the necessary steps to address the conflict can happen.

- **Active versus passive listening.** One key skill I encourage people to understand and apply is the ability to actively listen as opposed to passively listen. Passive listeners look like they are listening but they are simply waiting for an opportunity to respond. This can lead to a lack of communication and can further aggravate a conflict. Active listening, however, involves taking in and processing information from a place of understanding. Active listening allows you to really hear and focus on the issue at hand and weed out all of the emotions and assumptions that are preventing a resolution.

- **Be accountable.** In order to find a resolution in a conflict it is important to understand the role that you have played in the situation. In addition, in an effort to reach a resolution there will be some compromise and some letting go in order to move on. Take ownership of the things that you can control, namely your emotions and your actions, and work towards creating a healthier work environment.

- **Address issues face-to-face.** Nowhere is communication tested and assumptions made on a greater level than by e-mail, text, or other electronic communications. The reader fills in the blanks of tone, attitude, and emotion; he/she then responds based on their interpretation, whether accurate or not. Face-to-face communication is always the preferred method of communication when addressing conflict. If necessary, invite a supervisor or HR staff to provide support during this meeting to ensure that the focus is on resolution.

From personal experience, I repeatedly discovered that the source of conflict among staff revolved around receiving criticism. As an employer, it was my responsibility to hand down critiques of an employee's job performance as well as suggest areas of improvement. I have also been in the position where I have been on the receiving end of criticism. It is very easy to take criticism personally and feel like you are being attacked. Criticism is a necessary component for growth and evolution. No one is perfect and there is always room for improvement.

How can you possibly improve if you take criticism and insight on areas of need for improvement as a personal attack? You should embrace criticism and use it as a learning tool. Granted, if the criticism is not presented in a constructive and positive manner it can easily lead to conflict. If this happens it is important to understand that the lack of communication skills falls on the deliverer of the information instead of feeling like less of a person because you were critiqued. This issue should be addressed following the same approach detailed above.

Avoiding workplace conflict is ideal but very difficult to accomplish. Ignoring or avoiding conflict in that setting, and many others, will not make it go away and will often make things worse. It is important to actively resolve conflict when it arises and to do all you can to keep a healthy work environment. Remember, you do not have to be best friends with, or honestly even like, your co-workers. However, it is important for you to do your part to address conflict and handle your responsibilities effectively.

CHAPTER 15

PERSONAL BRANDING

"All of us need to understand the importance of branding. We are CEOs of our own companies: *Me Inc.* To be in business today, our most important job is to be head marketer for the brand called You."
- Tom Peters

Branding is everywhere. We are inundated with branding at every turn- from clothing, cars, and restaurants to so much more. We are so familiar with these labels and logos that we can identify these brands from a mile away. We have bestowed personal value and worth to these brands. We make conscious and subconscious decisions about what to buy, where to eat, or where to go based on the packaging and marketing of these brands. While the concept and practice of branding has long been associated with businesses and companies, personal branding carries great significance in the personal and professional world as well.

Personal branding is the practice of marketing yourself as a brand. The same way people associate the golden arches with McDonald's, the goal of personal branding is to leave a lasting impression in the minds of people so they associate you with various positive, professional, and career related values. The goal is to create a powerful, attractive, recognizable personal brand that carries significance in your industry and beyond. We have reached the point where it is no longer about if you have a personal brand but what your personal brand is and how do you continue to grow and develop it. The growth of social media opens new and creative ways of growing and expanding your personal brand as well.

When thinking of personal branding it is important to ask yourself what you want people to associate with your name. Do you want to be known for being knowledgeable about a specific topic and/or associated with general professional qualities? Once you have a greater sense of what you want your brand to look like then the planning begins on what needs to be done to develop that brand. The underlying premise is to portray the authentic version of you in a creative and unique way in order to come off as both genuine as well as innovative.

One of the best ways to start is with your personal story. Who are you? What are you about? What drives you as a person? What are your goals, dreams, and aspirations? What do you bring to the table and how can you help others? All of this information goes towards defining your brand. The best part is that the passion and energy will easily follow, as you are building something off of someone you know better than anyone else in the world- YOU!

Personal branding starts offline. Whether you know it or not, you already have a brand, whether it is a positive one or a negative one. Your character, integrity, and reputation all encompass your personal brand. Your brand includes how you dress, how you interact with people, your communication style, and even in your resume. It is about your level of trust, your honesty, and your values. If you really think about it this entire book is about developing your brand.

The great thing about personal branding is that we are completely in control. Every day we have an opportunity to control our brand in every interaction. As you grow and develop a positive, genuine offline brand, and as you increase your presence and visibility in the professional world, the transition to developing a powerful online brand will come naturally.

Online branding is a monster on its own and can be overwhelming but fun at the same time. For the purposes of this book, I want to target young and pre-professionals who are aiming to develop an online brand. Below are some helpful suggestions on how to begin the process of developing a powerful online presence while also finding ways to market yourself to influential professionals.

- **Review and adjust your current online presence.** While social media can serve as a powerful avenue to grow on a personal and professional level it can also ruin your brand. You must be very mindful of what you post on social media, ranging from pictures and posts to articles. Review your online content and ask yourself whether the material associated with you, that can easily be seen by anyone searching online, enhances your personal brand or negatively impacts it?

- **Create a LinkedIn account.** There is great value and potential for a young or pre-professional to develop a LinkedIn account. LinkedIn is a social network for professionals. It is an amazing avenue to not only grow our professional footprint but also connect with other professionals. LinkedIn allows you to use your profile as your resume, find and apply for jobs, connect with colleagues and new professionals, share information connected to your passion, and join professional groups.

- **Create a personal website.** A personal website is a fun and interactive way to control and share the content you wish to share with professionals. As you grow professionally, it can evolve into a multiple-page, service-offering, blog-sharing website that encompasses all that your brand is about. Until you reach that level, however, a website can contain your resume, your online social links, as well as a bio. You can always add to it as you grow.

- **Invest in headshots.** I have no doubt that people have tons of selfies and pictures with friends and families. Unfortunately, for the purposes of professional branding, they are not very helpful. I encourage young professionals to obtain a professional headshot which can be used as a profile picture on LinkedIn or even on a personal website.

- **Instagram, Twitter, Blog and Vlog.** Social media has a tremendous amount of potential to market a brand if done correctly. Sharing your story, sharing your passion, and showcasing your work are all critical ways to develop your brand and a powerful reputation. The important thing to keep in mind is consistency. Your message must be consistent with your brand and what you want to be known for and/or associated with. In addition, once you develop that solid Instagram page, or the insightful blog, make sure you market it to other professionals and people that will find it of interest. Network, connect, and plan strategically.

So, which is more important to invest in- the offline brand or the online brand? Lately, it seems like the development of an online brand far surpasses the need to develop an offline brand. This hints that there is some type of distinction between the two, when in fact there is no distinction other than how the branding takes place. The time and energy spent in developing and nurturing both will ultimately create a relationship where the offline brand will empower the online brand, and the online brand will empower the offline brand. It is critical to remember, however, that the image presented both online and offline must be of the same person. You should not falsely create an image online that will not translate when you present yourself in person.

Your online brand is most effective at extending your brand to people and avenues that you may otherwise not have access to. Sharing stories and testimonials or posting professional pictures of you at events will amplify your brand and reach new audiences while growing support in existing audiences. Offline branding will strengthen the connections and relationships that you have made with people, whether online or offline. Your reputation and brand in person will develop and strengthen in-person relationships, open doors to new opportunities, and grow your online presence.

The bottom line is that in order to effectively grow your brand, while increasing your presence and authority, you must focus on the genuine and strategic growth of both your online and offline brand. Become the next golden arches.

CHAPTER 16

QUOTES TO LIVE BY

I am a huge fan of insightful, inspirational, motivational, and empowering quotes. I can attempt to come up with clever and innovative ways of saying some really powerful things but sometimes you find those perfect words already stated. Each person is influenced or moved by a particular quote or the meaning behind a quote. With this in mind I wanted to share some of my favorite quotes in the hopes that can play a positive role in your life. If few or none of these quotes impact you I strongly advise that you look for quotes of your own to motivate you.

"Strive not to be a success, but rather to be of value."
-Albert Einstein

"Every strike brings me closer to the next home run."
-Babe Ruth

"A business that makes nothing but money is a poor business."
-Henry Ford

"Success is walking from failure to failure with no loss of enthusiasm."
-Winston Churchill

"It always seems impossible until it's done."
-Nelson Mandela

"Successful and unsuccessful people do not vary greatly in their abilities. They vary

in their desires to reach their potential."
-John Maxwell

"It's not what you achieve, it's what you overcome.
That's what defines your career."
-Carlton Fisk

"The bigger the dream, the harder the grind."
-Eric Thomas

"Work to become, not to acquire."
-Elbert Hubbard

"I've missed more than 9,000 shots in my career. I've
lost almost 300 games. 26 times, I've been trusted to
take the game winning shot and missed. I've failed over
and over and over again in my life.
And that is why I succeed."
-Michael Jordan

"You can't build a reputation on what you're going to
do."
-Confucius

"Focus your time on building meaningful relationships.
You can be the smartest person in the room, but if
nobody wants to work with you, that doesn't matter."
-Mogo

"Your attitude, not your aptitude,
will determine your altitude."
-Zig Ziglar

"The longer I live, the more I realize the impact attitude has on life. Attitude to me is more important than facts. It is more important than the past, than education, than money, than circumstances, than failures, than successes, than what other people think or say or do. It is more important than appearance, giftedness or skill. It will make or break a company…a church…a home. The remarkable thing is we have a choice everyday regarding the attitude we will embrace for the day. We cannot change our past. We cannot change the fact that people will act in a certain way. We cannot change the inevitable. The only thing we can do is play on the one string we have, and that is our attitude. I am convinced that life is 10% what happens to me and 90% how I react to it. And so it is with you.
We are in charge of our attitudes."
-Charles R. Swindoll

"You cannot climb the ladder of success dressed in the costume of failure."
-Zig Ziglar

"Don't make a habit of choosing what feels good over what is good for you."
-Eric Thomas

"Nothing succeeds like the appearance of success."
-Christopher Lasch

"You can tell the character of a person by their handshake."
-Kathy Magliato

"Your smile is your logo, your personality is your
business card, how you leave others feeling after having
an experience with you becomes your trademark."
-Anonymous

"Work like there is someone working twenty-four hours
a day to take it all away from you."
-Mark Cuban

"When you want to succeed, as bad as you want to
breathe, then you'll be successful."
-Eric Thomas

"You have an idea, a dream? Go for it, don't settle and
don't let anyone tell you that you can't –
opportunity is everywhere."
-Chrissy Sgourakis

"Be authentic, be you, and be the energy
you want to attract."
-Julia Hame

"Don't be afraid to take chances early on. The more
established you become within a particular field, the
harder it'll be to break free."
-Ash Molaei

"Be okay with failing. The traditional route isn't for
most of us. Learn from that failure and
carve your own path."
-Christian Dare

"The only way to get out of mediocrity is to keep
shooting for excellence."
-Eric Thomas

"It is literally true that you can succeed best and quickest by helping others to succeed."
-Napolean Hill

"The strongest thing that any human being has going for itself is its own integrity and it's own heart. As soon as you start veering away from that, the solidity that you need to stand up for what you believe in, just isn't going to be there."
-Herbie Hancock

"What lies behind us and what lies before us are small matters compared to what lies within us."
-Oliver Wendell Holmes

"Six essential qualities that are the key to success include sincerity, personal integrity, humility, courtesy, wisdom, and charity."
-Dr. William Menninger

"Whether you think you can, or you think you can't-- you're right."
-Henry Ford

"The future rewards those who press on. I don't have time to feel sorry for myself. I don't have time to complain. I'm going to press on."
-Barack Obama

"Be inspirational!"
-Richard Celestin

ABOUT THE AUTHOR

Richard Anthony Celestin was born and raised in Jamaica, Queens. He is living proof that adversity and obstacles can only strengthen and motivate us to achieve our dreams and goals. As a small child, he experienced severe bullying due to his height and weight. In high school, he had to overcome a life-changing medical diagnosis that resulted in his hospitalization, numerous surgical attempts to repair complications, and several near-death experiences. As a young professional, he lacked the focus and maturity to take advantage of the blessings that laid before him. Despite these odds Richard remained focused on achieving his dreams with the ultimate goal of giving back to his community and sharing his story and struggles as a source of inspiration.

Richard is a graduate of The City University of New York School of Law. While at CUNY Law, he focused his studies on criminal defense and juvenile justice. Prior to entering law school, and since becoming an attorney, he has directed his work towards underrepresented and at-risk youth via the not-for-profit sector and with alternative-to-detention programs in Manhattan, Brooklyn, and Queens. He offers his knowledge and insight into the juvenile and criminal justice areas by participating in panel discussions and conducting workshops throughout New York City addressing issues and concerns that affect communities of color, primarily the rising arrest and incarceration rates of youth of color.

In addition to working with youth involved in the juvenile and criminal justice systems, Richard created a limited liability corporation, Richard Celestin

102

Consulting Group, LLC, for the purposes of developing and providing legal skill development, self-awareness, youth empowerment, and consequential thinking programs to elementary, middle and high school students in Queens and Brooklyn. Under the LLC, Richard operates the Young Debaters Program, which has been implemented in over 40 schools and focuses on teaching students the skills behind debate and oral advocacy. Richard also serves as a consultant for various organizations seeking to develop youth-based programs within the community, practices various areas of the law, and is an adjunct professor at LaGuardia Community College and New York City College of Technology.

One of Richard's proudest moments to date is in the publication of his first book, *The Hard Facts About Soft Skills*. Knowing that his academic record was not sufficient to achieve the success he wanted and envisioned, Richard needed to develop and sharpen all the tools he had access to in order to remain competitive and relevant in the professional world. As with any successful person, it is imperative that he shares his journey and the valuable skills he learned along the way. As a proud author, Richard plans on publishing more works focused on personal and professional growth.

To learn more information about my work
and passion,
to book a speaking engagement or workshop,
or
to stay in contact,
please check out the following-

www.RichardCelestinLLC.com
RCelestinLLC@gmail.com
#youngdebatersprogram

www.TheInspirationalLawyer.com
TheInspirationalLawyer@gmail.com
IG: @the_inspirational_lawyer
#theinspirationallawyer

CPSIA information can be obtained
at www.ICGtesting.com
Printed in the USA
LVHW042331050123
736576LV00024B/579

9 781732 234109